Direct Work with
FAMILY
GROUPS

Direct Work with
FAMILY
GROUPS

SIMPLE, FUN IDEAS TO AID ENGAGEMENT AND ASSESSMENT AND ENABLE POSITIVE CHANGE

Audrey Tait and Helen Wosu

Jessica Kingsley *Publishers*
London and Philadelphia

First published in 2016
by Jessica Kingsley Publishers
73 Collier Street
London N1 9BE, UK
and
400 Market Street, Suite 400
Philadelphia, PA 19106, USA

www.jkp.com

Library of Congress Cataloging in Publication Data
A CIP catalog record for this book is available from the Library of Congress

British Library Cataloguing in Publication Data
A CIP catalogue record for this book is available from the British Library

ISBN 978 1 84905 554 3
eISBN 978 0 85700 986 9

Printed and bound in Great Britain

To all the families we have worked with who have challenged us, inspired us and continue to motivate us.

Contents

Chapter 1

Introduction

We would like to describe how we began our collaboration which first produced *Direct Work with Vulnerable Children* and now this book.

Audrey began her career as a nursery officer working with under 5s in children's centres. It was her first job and she was very young and inexperienced both in work and in life. She loved working with children and was just building up confidence when her supervisor told her that it was time she started to do some family work. She was very keen to begin but had no idea how to, or what 'family work' really meant. So she asked her supervisor, who posed a question back to her.

'What does John need from his mum that he is not getting right now?'

'Well…safe limits and boundaries and she needs to play with him.'

'Well, there you are,' she replied, 'That's what you need to teach his mum to do. That's family work – parenting support.'

Audrey was pleased she had got the answer right but still puzzled as to what to do. She began the way she knew best, by engaging children and their parents through activities which challenged some of their unhelpful and dysfunctional ways of thinking to bring change and hope.

For Helen it was a different route. After returning to Britain and social work after 20 years in Africa she found it very hard to reconcile the changes she saw and really struggled to find her feet again. For one thing she felt that clients no longer trusted social workers and for another the volume of paperwork and the constant changes in procedures and protocols seemed to make the job more stressful and harder. She also intuitively knew something was not right, especially when it came to helping children to have a voice. She began in a tentative way to introduce therapeutic storytelling in her practice and also to find ways of using the new information about how the brain functions[1] to inform the way she worked with vulnerable families. It was when she met Audrey (by then a qualified social worker with some years of practice under her belt) and saw the way she worked that it all fell into place.

Helen asked Audrey to lead a training course in 'Communicating with Children' for the Children and Families Department, City of Edinburgh Council. Both of us found newly qualified social workers had similar dilemmas to the ones we had faced. They told us often, 'They don't teach this stuff in university.'[2]

More experienced workers have also appreciated learning new ways of working with families and rebuilding trust and respect and have incorporated these into their repertoire of resources, reigniting their enthusiasm for working with families. One worker told us after attending a training day, 'This is reclaiming social work. It is why I came into the job.'

Audrey and Helen suspect that many more people feel a similar way. They have been heartened by the positive response to their first book, Direct Work with Vulnerable Children. They hope that this book gives you some ideas for working with family groups to help with the question, 'How?' It is not set out to be academic per se and the activities described in this book are not difficult to do. There are many excellent books written around the theory of working with families and the authors would encourage you to read them. Those of you who have studied these will recognise the academic theories underpinning these activities. This book is intended to focus on the practical to complement the theory: to give you ideas for practical activities which will aid in building up relationships, inform your assessments and begin those 'big conversations' that can be so hard to start but which can often bring healing and change.

---

1   See Gerhardt, S. (2004) Why Love Matters. Hove: Routledge and Ratey, J. (2001) A User's Guide to the Brain. London: Little Brown.

2   As Audrey's work became more recognised, even teachers and a community police officer came to her for advice on how to build relationships with young people.

As in *Direct Work with Vulnerable Children* the majority of the activities are from Audrey's bag, written in her voice and edited and compiled by Helen. In this book they wanted to include some of the excellent work they have come across by others, and they have used the names of the contributors with their permission.

The anonymous practice examples included here will give voice, the authors hope, to the families we all work with, who often show great courage in the face of adversity.

Below are a couple of quotes from parents. The first is from a parent whose children were removed from her care without her consent and then rehabilitated back home after two years; the second is from a grandmother whose grandchildren were placed on the Child Protection Register as a direct result of her referral to social services.

'You kind of took us all apart and then stuck us back together again. I hated you, but we are better for it. I am clean from the drugs and the bairns [children] are happier. I think the thing I remember most is you [Audrey] and that big F-----g bag ! I used to dread it. I couldnae believe some of the stuff but I did it and we had a laugh and the kids and I kind of always got on better for a wee while afterwards.'

'I didn't want to phone you because you hear all these stories about children getting taken away but it couldn't go on the way it was. I am glad I phoned now. You caused loads of grief but the kids liked you and then Gemma [daughter] began to listen and things got sorted. I never thought I would see Gemma using star charts and baking with the kids. It's good.'

Hold these in your heart as you go into the community and create positive change through direct work.

Chapter 2

The First Home Visit

No matter what your role is with the family, the first home visit is very important. It is a crucial moment, a time you won't ever recapture. Not only are you getting the first impressions of the family but they are doing the same of you. The adult family members will be making an assessment of you and this is more than likely formed not so much on what they see but on their previous experiences and what they may have heard from peers or neighbours. It is not uncommon to be faced with resistance or lack of engagement before you even get to say hello. This may be born out of fear and anxiety or a cultural belief that authority, in any form, is to be resisted.

We always apply the 'stage not age' principle to adults as well as children, as they can also be stuck developmentally. The first interactions may give you a clue as to where the adult is developmentally and help you to gauge your responses. Meeting a 50-year-old who is stuck at adolescence has not been an uncommon experience for us, but we have equally been faced with behaviour more reminiscent of a 3-year-old. It is important to point out that most people presenting in this way will have fragmented development. That is to say not every one area of development will be stuck or delayed. Most commonly we see issues embedded in their emotional and social development.

The children in the family will be making their own assessment of you too. The younger the child, the more they will be watching the reactions of their parents for clues about you. Do Mum and Dad like you? Can I approach you safely? Do you look fun? Are you interested in me?

Older children will be wondering how to behave around you. Are you going to take them away? Are they in big trouble? How far can they push boundaries? Do you have anything to offer them? Are you safe? Often these questions stem from what adults have told them about professionals. It is not uncommon for children to be threatened with, 'I'll get the social worker to come and take you away!'

Your reactions to their surroundings will also be absorbed unconsciously if not consciously. How do you respond to their pet? Do you acknowledge the presence of all the members of the family? Do you look shocked? (There is a difference between a concerned and a shocked look, but remembering that those with a history of poor parenting often find facial expressions hard to assess correctly it is better to adopt a friendly but neutral expression.)

At a recent event in Edinburgh where children were invited to review their experiences of being on the Child Protection Register one child said he 'felt invisible' when his social worker visited. It takes skill and practice to avoid this as many parents dominate the time with the worker. Be aware of this dynamic and actively ensure the child is included appropriately.

First visits can sometimes be tense and awkward, depending on the reason for the visit, but the more you can appear relaxed, at ease and not in a hurry to get away, the better you will help the family to relax. Their observations of you in those first few minutes can make a big impact and stay with them for a long time. Be aware of your body language. Remember you are a visitor (albeit sometimes an unwelcome one) to their home and behave accordingly. You may wish to verbalise your value base, being explicit. I often talk about respect in the first visit.

It is more than likely that you are there to make a first assessment of the family and home. Audrey likes to use the PILES approach as a starting point as she started out as a nursery nurse where this is used. It also fits well with the Department of Health Triangle and the Scottish 'My World Triangle', an assessment tool for gathering information about the child.[1]

The PILES approach looks at Physical, Intellectual, Language, Emotional and Social areas of a child's life and development. It takes all one's skills to get as much from the first visit as you can (by

---

1   See www.gov.scot/Topics/People/Young-People/gettingitright/national-practice-model/my-world-triangle.

16

observation), whilst also laying the foundation for building a trusting relationship with the family. A sound knowledge of child development is critical here as you begin to assess the child, the parents' ability to meet the child's needs and the environment of the home.

- Listen to the language the adults use around the children and to describe the children. In the American assessment tool, 'The Home Inventory', they suggest you make two or three positive comments about the child while you are in the home and gauge the reaction of the parent. Do they express pleasure or warmth when hearing the comments or try to kill the praise with a rebuttal?

- Watch their interactions with the children whilst you are there. Is the parent able to keep the child/children in mind while also talking to you? What is their tone of voice? Are they able to maintain control? A word of caution here. If you are a new visitor it is likely the parents will be anxious, especially if you are there because of childcare concerns. Children react to parents' behaviour and they could pick up the vibes and be reacting to this. Also remember most children will 'play up' when there is a new person around, especially if that person is taking the parents' attention away from them.

It may not be possible to cover all the indicators needed to assess the home on this first visit. Unless concerns are so heightened that the immediate accommodation of the child has to be considered, priority should be given to establishing a working relationship with the family whilst using your observation skills.

To give an indication of the kind of detail you need to be looking for in order to make a good assessment, we give examples of how we would gather evidence in the different areas.

Physical environment

- Before you enter, have a good look at the outside environment. How safe is it for a child? Is there stuff dumped in the garden which could create risk (old refrigerators; barbed wire; broken glass). Is there CCTV? If it is a block of flats, is there a concierge? Is the block well maintained?

- Once inside, is it clean enough? There is a difference between cleanliness and untidiness. Dog faeces or dirty nappies on the floor pose risk to health and you need to address that immediately. Evidence of food that has been lying around for more than a day is unhygienic. Piles of papers, clothes or toys scattered around is untidiness. If it is so cluttered that a toddler cannot negotiate their way safely around the home, this needs to be addressed relatively quickly.

- Are there any objects lying around that could pose risk to a child, remembering young children move around at floor level?

- Are the floors safe? Look for trip hazards, but also be mindful to watch out for moving (or missing) floor boards. Audrey once visited a home where there were floor boards missing as the family had burnt some of the floor boards in order to provide heat.

- Is there adequate bedding? Touch the sheets to see if they are dry.

- Does the child have access to drinks? Are they given in an appropriate bottle/cup for their age? If not, why not? Parents may not know enough about child development or they may simply not possess the right cup.

- Are medicines stored safely? If there is a known drug or methadone user in the family, where do they store what they use?

- Are there safety catches on windows with the keys removed from the locks? Same with the main door. Very young toddlers can learn early to open doors.

- Is there any evidence of vermin?

- Do plugs have safety sockets fitted? Are the plugs themselves safe – not hanging out of the walls?

- Is there evidence of more people living there than you know about (e.g. the pair of men's shoes sitting under a table in a home where the man was supposed to be out of the house for safety reasons)?

- Is there a chain on the door?

- Can you smell cannabis, alcohol, damp?

- Is there a building entry system and does it work?

- If there are pets, how well are they cared for? (Research suggests a strong correlation between abuse/neglect of children and of animals.)

- Is there a fire guard? Are the radiators safe to touch?

- Is there a smoke alarm?

Physical development

- Does the child look clean, dirty, have ingrained dirt? What is the condition of their hair? It may be messy, which is not necessarily a problem (unless this makes the child look significantly scruffier than their peers which may attract negative comments), but does it look matted or sticky? Are there head lice? (Having head lice is very common. It is only an indicator of neglect when a parent does not check regularly for head lice and does not treat head lice.)

- Does the child have their own personal space where they sleep/ keep their toys? Children should be able to access at least some of their toys without needing adult help.

- Babies and toddlers need special attention as their physical needs have to be met in a timely way or their health could deteriorate rapidly. Are they changed frequently enough? (If you suspect this is a problem ask how many nappies they use in a day; enquire about their routine.) Does the child have a nappy rash and, if so, what is being done to treat it? If the rash is bad and not responding to treatment, they must see their doctor or health visitor. It is a very painful condition for babies; the condition itself is not rare but there should be evidence of care and ongoing treatment.

- For babies, create an opportunity to be around when a bottle is being made up or during feeding. Consider the parent's attention to hygiene. It is always worth observing meal time with any age of child. How hungry are they? What are the portion sizes? Consider food hygiene and nutrition.

- What is the state of the child's health in general? Do they have any ongoing condition and is it being attended to regularly? You will look for information from the parent, from the child if old enough and from health professionals. The latter's opinion on ongoing health issues is vitally important.

- Is the child's development age-appropriate? The brain makes vital connections for motor skills in the first two years of life. Poor stimulation and few opportunities to be active during this developmental window can affect a child for life. Babies who are tied in buggies whilst in the home (to make caring easier for parents) can be significantly delayed in gross motor skills. Look at the baby's head. If it is very flat at the back it *may* be an indicator of 'buggy baby', so ask for a paediatric assessment.

- Are the child's clothes fit for purpose and appropriate for the season? Are they the right size, especially the shoes? Are clothes soiled and smelly? Find out if this is a chronic problem or a temporary one due to circumstances (washing machine broken; adults unwell etc.) A child should not be left in a state of neglect, which is a form of abuse and can affect a child's self-esteem and socialisation.

- In the case of older children is their clothing stored in a way that helps them to be independent in choosing what to wear? Sadly it is really common for clothes to be in such disarray that the child can't find a full set of clothes.

Intellectual development

- Is understanding age-appropriate?

- Are there any memory issues? This is not uncommon with parents who have a history of drug and/or alcohol abuse.

- Are there any learning difficulties?

- Is there developmental delay?

- Does the child show curiosity? Are they interested in new experiences?

- Has the parent provided play materials/equipment and are they within reach of the child to allow for spontaneous play?

- Does the parent support play appropriately? You are looking for a combination of play materials; space to play; joining in play; leaving the child to play independently; letting the child lead play and supporting this by capitalising on learning opportunities. For example, the child plays at 'shop' and invites the parent to join in. The parent does and in their play together encourages counting, 'I'll have three buns please,' or for the older child playing with toy money and counting this out.

- Is there good attendance and timekeeping at nursery? Or school? If not, why not?

- Is there access to books at home?

- Does the parent support homework?

- Does the parent have good links with school? Do they communicate with the teacher; attend parents' evenings; show interest in the child's learning?

- Is the child organised for school? Does the parent support them with this?

- Is an advocacy worker required?

- How is the parent's money management? Do they need help with bills; tenancy agreements; legal process?

- How does the parent's development compare with the child's? Is there an appropriate gap or is the child more than or as able as the parent? If so how is this impacting on the relationship and how are the child's learning needs being met?

Language development

- What is the family's first language? Is an interpreter required?

- Is the child's verbal ability age-appropriate?

- Is the child's understanding of language age-appropriate? If not, why not? Could there be a hearing problem or a specific learning disability?

- Can the child communicate effectively? Most parents will understand their child's gestures and language which others may not be able to understand. If this isn't the case I would be curious about that.

- Does the parent listen to the child?

- Is the child able to take turns in the conversation?

- How is the parent's written language? Can they read and write?

- Is the child's drawing and writing age-appropriate?

- Are they given the opportunity to draw/write – are the materials to do this available? Children should have access to crayons and paper from 12 months. Research tells us that the earlier a child begins to enjoy making marks on paper the more success they will have in reading and writing later.

- Is the child's reading age-appropriate?

- Does the child read regularly and/or have stories read to them daily?

- Do they have their own books readily available to them? You may be able to help the family join the library.

- Note the words a young child uses for objects and body parts etc. They may have their own words for some favourite objects, like the toddler who called her dummy her 'newt newt'. As it turned out this was very good to know because when I had to place her with carers under stressful circumstances I was able to tell the carer what her 'newt newt' was.

- Watch out for parents/carers who give the child a dummy or bottle constantly. This will negatively affect the child's language development, as well as their dental health.

- Does the parent use rhymes and songs? This is very important for language development. In older children look for the use of poetry, funny rhymes and games with words. This may seem very basic to you and it is. However, it affects a child's academic future and every child has the right to education; we need to support parents to get the foundations in place. Exposure to language in the home is essential. The number of words a child hears during their second year significantly affects the child's vocabulary for the rest of their life.[2] Parents don't need to be able to read to sing a song or recite a poem. You can model it for them. It only takes five minutes out of your visit and what's more helps with relationship building.

Practice example

Dave was a single parent to Claire (4). I noticed that there were no books or newspapers in the home, just advertising leaflets. I queried this gently and Dave explained he couldn't read so there was no point in having them in the home. I said to him that I bet he knew a nursery rhyme and he shyly admitted that he knew a few and Claire liked them. I further found out that each night they went through all the rhymes they knew, so the next week I brought a book of nursery rhymes and before we knew it we were connecting pictures to rhymes and occasional words to pictures. Dave and Claire joined the local public library and I showed Dave how to picture-read, advising him to stick to traditional stories first – the ones he knew from his childhood. Claire loved Dad reading her stories and it became very much part of their daily routine.

When Claire started school, Dave initially asked Granny to collect her from school and do her homework with her, but he eventually decided he wanted to do this and so he attended adult literacy classes.

---

2   Ratey, J. (2001) *A User's Guide to the Brain*. London: Little, Brown and Company.

Emotional development

- Is there warmth in the parent/child relationship?

- What is the attachment between the child and parent? Remember attachment behaviour only shows when the child is anxious, fearful or distressed so you may be asking the parent, 'What does [child] do when he [falls down and hurts himself; is hungry and tired etc.]?' as well as using your observation skills. All you can hope to do is develop a hypothesis which you test by asking as many people as possible what their observations are. Assessing attachment certainly isn't something you can do in just one visit but as you get to know the family and talk to others you will be able to develop some idea of where your intervention needs to be focused.

- How does the parent react when you compliment the child? Your compliment might be based on something the parent has told you about the child or your own observations as long as it is sincere and accurate.

- Does the parent praise the child?

- Does the parent have reasonable expectations for the child's developmental stage?

- Does the parent set consistent boundaries? Does the child feel contained? Do they have appropriate sanctions for developmental stage *and* the severity of the misdemeanour?

- Does the parent have positive expectations of the child?

- Does the parent show respect for the child? Do they value their opinions and views? This doesn't mean they have to act on them.

- Does the parent have protective feelings for the child?

- Does the parent give the child age-appropriate levels of responsibility? Do they maintain the parental role and not stray into treating the child as a peer?

- Does the parent promote the child's self-esteem/sense of worth? This won't be easy or natural for many parents but as a basic you need to see acknowledgement that the child has a right to feel good about himself and see that the parent is willing to try and promote this.

- Is the parent careful not to decry an absent or abusive partner with whom the child still has a relationship?

- Is the parent aware of dynamics in the sibling group and do they try to manage this so that each child has their needs met? Is there a sense of the parent being fair?

- Are promises kept? A child should not have to suffer multiple disappointments for no logical or explained reason. Some parents emotionally abuse children by deliberately promising things and then taking them away.

- Is the child's space well maintained – or at least as well maintained as the adult's space – with clothes and toys respected and cared for? Children need help to keep their room in order right into the teenage years.

- Does the parent make time to spend with their child doing something the child likes?

- What are the parental expectations around meal times, personal care and bedtimes? You want to see recognition of needs and willingness to give care.

- Does the parent offer the child emotional support?

- Is the parent able to recognise that their child needs wider social contacts outside the family to effectively meet their emotional needs and are the parents willing to promote the child's relationships with others?

- Is the parent sensitive to the child's vulnerabilities?

- Does the parent accept the child's range of emotions and allow expression of these? If not, why not? How does this influence the parenting skills?

- Is the parent able to protect their child from their own emotions? For example, is a parent able to protect their child from loud/ aggressive adult arguments or from extreme distress? In every family there are a range of emotions displayed which is part of learning to cope with feelings. However, children should not be exposed to parents who are out of control on a regular basis.

Social development

- Is the child's social development age-appropriate?
- Are they being supported to have positive social experiences, for instance interaction with peers and other adults?
- Are they regularly taken out? Even young babies need to be taken out for walks in their prams and have opportunities to meet other people.
- Are older children supported to have friendships and allowed an age-appropriate level of independence? For younger children this would mean being toilet trained at the right age and stage; being allowed to feed themselves at the weaning stage and mess tolerated. For older children, it could mean being allowed to play independently in the garden; to walk home from school with friends. For teenagers it may be appropriate coming-home times.
- Does the parent teach socially acceptable behaviour?
- Does the parent support the child and encourage them to access services in the community – parks; library; community centre; medical centre; police etc.
- Does the parent model good citizenship and community involvement?

Some practice wisdom on the use of interpreters

It is only relatively recently that I have had a need to use interpreters. It has been a bit of a learning curve for me so I thought it may be helpful to share these points:

- When asking a family what their first language is, also ask what the preferred dialect is.
- Avoid family members interpreting for each other, for obvious reasons, that is, you don't know if the interpretation is accurate and if there is honesty between each family member.

• Be aware that there may be issues of confidentiality, perceived or real. I worked with an Asian woman who had some English but was not confident in the language. I wanted to use an interpreter to ensure that she understood the information about child protection proceedings. She was adamant she didn't want me to access interpretation services. Eventually she explained that the Asian community was very connected and insisted that the interpreter would tell one of the senior members of her immediate family about the child protection issue and this would bring shame on her and her family. I tried to reassure her about the professionalism of the interpreter service but she was unconvinced. Real or perceived, this issue was a barrier.

• When working with an interpreter, double your interview time!

• I find people appreciate it if you try to learn even one word of their language. A simple greeting is all you need.

Chapter 3

Keeping Yourself Safe

Safety is an increasingly big issue but it helps to consider that thousands of home visits are made every day with no problems. Even so, we are likely to be going into unfamiliar environments and many of those we visit have vulnerabilities that can potentially create risk. Some clients we visit will have learnt that the best form of defence is aggression. They could be involved in crime and as a consequence there could be weapons in the property.

Some people engage in risk-taking behaviour and many own potentially dangerous pets (it seems to be my luck to meet more of these than I would like to). So with all this in mind, here are some ways we have learnt over the years to decrease risk and increase safety:

- Prior to leaving your workplace, make sure you sign out correctly, leaving the address you are visiting, the name of the family and expected return time.

- If you think the risk is higher than normal, either insist on making a joint visit with a colleague, or arrange with a colleague to phone them when you arrive at the property and when you leave.

- Make sure you have a mobile phone with you, but watch that you don't have a false sense of security as they can be (and have been in our experience) taken from you. Also make sure it is charged and in a place you can reach easily, not at the bottom of a cluttered bag.

- If driving, park as near as possible to the address and if there is CCTV in the area, see if you can park in its view. When dark, try to park under or near street lighting. Keep your car keys where they are quickly and easily accessible.

- When visiting property with a concierge, introduce yourself. In my experience they are always helpful and don't mind watching out for you.

- Use the lifts as they have cameras, whereas the stairways usually do not.

- When you knock, try to give a friendly knock, then step back so that the service user can see you without feeling oppressed and vice versa. If there is a spy hole in the door, stand in view of that and wear your ID where it can be seen.

- If there is no bell or knocker and you have to rattle the letterbox, use your diary or other implement – not your fingers – just in case there is an enthusiastic dog on the other side.

- Always carry a torch – nowadays many mobile phones have torches but I prefer something a little more robust that can light up a stairway. Many of the places we visit have long hallways, often cluttered and unlit. Also if a client switches off the lights suddenly or if there is a power cut you are covered.

- When the door is opened be confident and engaging right from the start.

- You may want to request that dogs be put in another room or outside if possible.

- As you move into the house, glimpse into any rooms where doors are open so you are aware if anyone else is around, as well as getting a first impression of the state of the property. If you can hear someone but can't see them, at an appropriate moment ask the client who else is in the home as you are concerned about confidentiality (and of course your own safety).

- As you enter, note the exits. There may be only one – the way you came in – and you have to factor that into where you sit – preferably somewhere with a direct line to the door.

- Note the type of lock on the door and how it works.

- Before sitting, ask where they would like you to sit and then check quickly for sharp objects or pets. Sit on the edge of the chair if possible. A client once deliberately sat Audrey on a seat which had a large snake curled down the back and which slowly emerged during conversation. Luckily she likes snakes!

- Try to keep everyone in your sight. Invite all family members to join you, especially on the first visit. Work out where the power lies in the family group and direct your initial efforts of engagement to that person and try to establish mutual respect and boundaries. Do pay attention to family members' cues as to family hierarchy as they know each other best.

- Lastly, trust your instincts. If something *feels* wrong then you are probably right. Never hesitate to end a home visit prematurely if you are beginning to feel unsafe. It is better for the client and for you that you leave before anything goes wrong: 'I think we need to leave it there for today. Thank you for your time, I'll be in touch.'

Chapter 4

What to Do If You Don't Get Access – The Client Refuses to Open the Door

Getting access to a family home is extremely important if there are concerns about the welfare of a child. If at all possible one should try to get access without alienating the family even further, and we acknowledge this can be very hard. But our clients have learned to be very wary of strangers and quite creative in their acts of avoidance. The most effective form of avoidance is usually non-engagement in the hope that the pressure will reduce and eventually cease.

We can't allow this to happen where there are vulnerable children so here are some of our ideas, based on experience.

The obvious thing to do is put a note through the door with another appointment date. If, after several attempts to engage with the client, this doesn't work, you could try some of the following ideas:

- Carefully open the letterbox and shine your torch through. The light may attract a child to come and investigate. If so, engage them in conversation or sing a nursery rhyme; perhaps play with a puppet to establish that you are friendly and fun. Then ask about their mum and dad. Where are they? What are they doing?

- Consider carefully before asking them to go and get them. If the child asks who you are, give them your first name and explain what you do. Avoid giving a job title as this may not mean much to them, or they may have been told scary things about social workers/family care workers. Tell the child you will come back later – giving a time later in the day or another day that suits you. Do this even if the child is too young to understand as the parent may be listening. Make your next visit as soon as possible as you are trying to establish rapport with your client. If that turns out to be another letterbox conversation, have fun again. I sometimes bring bubbles and try to blow them through the letterbox. This creates lots of hilarity and this sometimes brings a curious parent to the door, or sometimes the child will open the door to get to the bubbles. If this happens, don't be tempted to enter the property but carry on with the play and encourage the child to go and get Mum and Dad. I have placed something to jam the door open at this point, but would never enter as this could be unsafe and local law where you live may very well count this as an offence.

- Do be prepared to have letterbox conversations with adults too. Be friendly; explain you want to work with them. Ask about previous experience of meeting helping agencies. Try the 'the sooner I am in – the sooner I am away' argument.

- If you haven't been able to establish a conversation through the letterbox, try sending a nice card to the child, a picture postcard with something appealing to children. The idea is to engage the child but also give the whole family a chance to see your non-threatening side. You could write something like:

  'Hello Joe,

  My name is X and I am looking forward to meeting you and your mum. I am a safe adult who helps look after boys and girls. Your teacher told me you like cars. I like them too and have a little blue car. Maybe you can show me your toy cars when I visit. I will see you on Monday at 3.45pm just after school closes.'

  Sign off with your name and a photo of yourself if you feel that's appropriate.

- Of course you can also send a formal letter too and offer to meet the family in the community.

- Get in touch with other professionals who know the family to help introduce you to them, and they may also be able to help you find out what the problem is. If the family feel they have had a bad experience of social services before, acknowledge this when you do meet. You may also be able to arrange a visit with someone the family already knows, such as a child health worker.

- Text messages are used more than letters now but be careful what you say as you don't know who might be reading them. If I am still trying to make contact with a reluctant client I might say I am following up a recent letter I sent to them, without putting my full name and job title. Once I have established a relationship, I usually say that I only use texts to confirm dates and times of visits.

- Most importantly – just persist with frequent visits and letters.

Chapter 5

Once in the Door

This part is to some degree difficult to write as there are so many variables. Always remember your safety and risk reduction behaviour (see Chapter 3) and you will of course have an idea in your head of what you aim to achieve – usually to make an initial assessment.

So, let's focus on the task of engaging the family.

The child first

- First and foremost, the child's needs come first and so my focus will be on the child (or children) as they are the most important people in the room from my perspective and my acknowledgement of the presence of the children in a friendly and child-focused way will convey the message to the parent in an obvious and visual way. It also allows the parent/carer to judge me and, I hope, find me unthreatening and interested.

- Complimenting the child gives an insight into the quality of the parent/child relationship. Compliments ignored or denied will raise your concerns. If received well they may help reduce any tensions in the carer about your visit.

- For some children, your immediate attention helps reduce their anxiety and so they may settle more easily when you begin the work with the adults and be more easily distracted into occupational play. You can begin to set boundaries and routine. 'I am going to play with you and then talk to Mummy and you can play on your own for a while. Then I'll play with you again. Okay?' This gives parameters and sets out what is going to happen. It can be helpful for both the child and the adult because it provides a sense of predictability and therefore increases feelings of safety.

• When starting to engage with a child, don't be tempted to use a barrage of questions, 'What is your favourite colour? Which football team do you support? What is your favourite TV programme?' These may seem harmless but it can seem threatening to a child who may have been warned of your visit and told not to say anything (remember children are very literal). This form of engagement can confirm that you are going to interrogate them and the adults in the room may feel anxious about how you will interpret the information. It also places the child in the position of having to give a bit of themselves to you before they have had time to assess you.

• Instead you need to be in a position where *you* entertain *them*, where you can convey a non-threatening interest in them and let them lead the interaction. So, how to do this? It will vary enormously depending on age and stage of development and to some degree the environment (see Table 5.1).

TABLE 5.1: A GUIDE FOR DEVELOPMENTALLY APPROPRIATE ACTIVITIES

Under 5 years	Middle childhood	Adolescents
Entertain: use a song or a story from your bag; a bottle of soap bubbles; a teddy or other toy from your bag. Convey interest: give full attention; good eye contact; lots of smiles; reflect back what they are doing.	Entertain: have some figures of favourite characters; a book of photos; a small, quick craft activity; bring pens and paper. Convey interest: give full attention; listen carefully; compliment their ideas; maybe ask about a logo on their T-shirt.	Entertain: tell them a funny story about yourself; ask their advice or opinion on a subject they are likely to know something about; offer a small craft activity; let them listen to music on your iPhone. Convey interest: give full attention; listen carefully; compliment their ideas; maybe ask about a logo on their T-shirt.

As far as you can, get them to lead the interaction, so if they bring you a toy, play with that; if they start to talk about music, go with that. I also often carry small snacks with me which I might share with them and the parent with the parent's permission. I believe in the powerful positive emotions which can be tapped into by the sharing of food and drink and so use it a lot in my work. It sends a message of care and concern and gives them another reason to stay engaged with me.

The parents' turn

One of the biggest challenges here can be coping with the children while you speak to the adults. Sending children under 12 years old out of the room is unlikely to work. If it does I might even be inclined to worry, although there are always exceptions. Teenagers on the other hand rarely want to stay (but may listen at the door).

So what does this mean?

- At this point children should have enjoyed your company and therefore not want to give up time with you.

- Children are naturally curious and want to be where the action is.

- Very young children should want to be near or in sight of their attachment figure. If that person is feeling anxious themselves, this is likely to trigger attachment behaviour in the child and we have to remember that most of the children we visit will not have secure attachments.

- Children know their parents well. They may be worried about the impact of your visit on the parent's behaviour. They may feel they need to be present to see if you are going to make Mum angry or upset. They will know the consequence of this even if you do not at this stage. It could mean that they may be at risk of being hit; or being emotionally abused. Or the parent may take drugs or alcohol to cope and present scary behaviour.

So, it may not be a good idea for the children to be sent out of the room.

- Take control by offering an occupational play activity that will entertain them in the same room. Paper and pens, small world toys (Playmobil, LEGO etc); anything that encourages solitary play and has high entertainment value. Even older children will enjoy using your pens which will be good quality and your paper and maybe some stamps or stickers too. Maybe you have a small electronic game they can play with. If you can look after the kids it will help the parent/carer to focus on the conversation.

- If there is a small child in the parent's arms you can get them to focus on you. Maybe you have a finger puppet which keeps popping out of your pocket as you talk, or perhaps you can keep handing them small toys or playing a finger game with them as you have an adult conversation.

- Reassure the parent when necessary. All children have a tendency to act up when there is an audience. It is very normal but stressful for parents especially when it is someone who is assessing them who is visiting. Tell them you realise this and no parent has the perfect child or gets it right all the time. It is probably more of a warning if you meet a child who is exceptionally good throughout the visit.

- Remember you can't complete an assessment in just one visit. Even if it is a high tariff visit (perhaps as a result of a report of serious concerns), it still can only be an initial assessment. This should always be informed by the opinions of others who know the family. So give yourself the permission to do the best you can to give the child and the family a good experience and to do no harm.

- If you do become aware of immediate risk or urgent need during your visit, you have to discuss this with the parent there and then and indicate you will be taking these concerns back to your manager.

Chapter 6

Working with Resistance, Challenging Behaviour and Aggression

Working with families who are struggling is not easy. If they were very self-aware, motivated to change, resilient and with positive self-esteem they wouldn't need help. But the reality is that most of the adults we work with do not self-refer but have been mandated by one means or another to work on issues which concern the children in their care. So in this context resistance is to be expected and may even be a normal reaction to being pushed to change.

Also many of the people who make up the families in our caseloads have experienced abusive situations, know what it feels like to be powerless or have lived with cruelty, unkindness and fear. These experiences create survivors and these survivors have learned how to cope, how to defend themselves and how to survive in an uncertain and scary world. They have built up coping strategies just to get by and get enough safety and attention to get through life as they experience it.

Unfortunately many of these strategies are unhelpful. They may be self-limiting or even damaging to themselves or to people around them, but because of their familiarity and the feelings of being in control they can bring, they are held on to with tenacity. A metaphor might be hanging on to a raft full of nails when floundering at sea and not being aware that the nails are tearing the skin. Without the raft, we drown. Without the coping strategies – the behaviours – life would be just too scary and anxiety-ridden to contemplate. Helping a family to make a positive change can be hard work for you and the family. But the satisfaction of being part of the process makes the work worthwhile.

Recognising resistance

How do we work with these unhealthy coping strategies? First we need to recognise them for what they are. Sometimes this is easy to spot. A door slammed in the face; repeated no shows; verbal aggression; the circular conversations going nowhere; responses like 'I've tried that before'; absolute denial of any problems or of any responsibility for children's behaviour and so on. But often it is more subtle, as in the parent who appears to engage, be willing to work with you and be motivated for change but no change comes. Or the client who does just enough to alleviate immediate concerns, who presents well but there is no evidence of positive change in concerns you have for the child/children.

We need to be able to identify resistance and accept it as part of this family's usual protective response to any outside challenge before we can understand it and help them to feel safe enough to let it go.

Practice example

Mags was a 30-year-old single parent with two boys aged 10 and 8 respectively. She had a strong personality and sense of direction in her life and had been brought up in a family with a strong work ethic. There was a history of short-term social work intervention. When her eldest child was a baby she had taken him to work with her, and this environment had posed risks to the baby. Also there had been further referrals around lack of supervision and queries as to whether she was misusing prescription drugs.

An accident in the home, when the younger child was injured, brought social work attention again and Audrey was allocated the case.

The first few visits and telephone calls brought no response, so Audrey began daily unannounced visits. On the third or fourth attempt she got a response. The door was opened and shut in her face, accompanied with verbal abuse. Audrey remained outside the door while she wrote and posted a note through the letterbox, deliberately framing it in a friendly tone, saying she would be back again. Her judgement was that Mags' behaviour was 'storm and bluster', designed to try to manipulate the situation rather than be overtly threatening.

The following day Audrey did a further visit and the door was opened to Mags shouting at her – the gist of it being she didn't like social workers on her doorstep. Then she turned and walked into the house, leaving the door open. Audrey waited for the invitation to come in, 'Are you no fucking coming in then?' and followed her into the sitting room, where she spotted the two boys trying to hide behind the television. She acknowledged them with a smile and wave before they ducked further down behind the television.

After this brief period of calm, Mags began her verbal assault again. Audrey, keeping her exit clear should it be needed, took the onslaught full on while steadying herself with a hand on the back of the settee. This went on for about five minutes, during which time Audrey was keeping an eye on the two boys. When it began to subside a little and Audrey noticed the boys had stood up again, she pulled a finger puppet out from her pocket and began to engage the boys with the puppet's antics. At the same time Mags was giving her space to begin to empathise with her and reflect back some of her statements. Eventually the boys laughed and at this point Mags became aware of the play, 'What the fuck are you doing?' and the boys tensed up again.

Audrey: 'Just playing. Would you like a go?'

Mags, unsurprisingly, refused the puppets and continued her conversation while Audrey listened and continued with the finger play. Although unable to give the boys undivided attention, Audrey was acknowledging their presence and sending a message that she was child-centred and fun.

Mags eventually began to relax. Her breathing calmed down, her speed slowed and she was beginning to let Audrey into the conversation. At this point Audrey judged it was time to leave. She was aware that the visit was causing anxiety and the children had had a stressful 30 minutes. They were very watchful of Mum and Audrey wanted to end the visit on a positive note. She explained she would have to go and made an appointment to return. When Mags went to get the calendar to mark the time and date of the next visit, Audrey recognised she had achieved a degree of co-operation.

Before she left, Audrey spoke to the boys directly and thanked them for letting her speak to their mum, inviting them to come and get a sticker from her. The purpose of this was to get them to feel safe enough to come to her (increase proximity); leave behind a small transitional object (the sticker) and from a behavioural perspective reward them for the effort/emotional strain of the past 30 minutes. Also Mags was watching and she hoped on some level Mags was processing her behaviour towards the boys and would model it herself.

Dealing with challenging situations and aggression

When facing a situation which is more challenging, never place yourself at risk and do follow your employer's guidelines and policy on keeping safe. If you have never seen or read these guidelines, maybe this is the time to do it.

It is never wise to ignore any signals that the situation is not safe, even if you feel you know the person well. 'I'm going now, and will contact you or you can call me, when you are feeling calmer' stated in a moderate, non-accusatory tone followed by a swift retreat is always the best policy.

However, sometimes the situation gets heated after you have entered the home. The following are additional tips and skills the authors have found helpful:

• See it for what it is – behaviour. It is rarely personal but is a response to fear of perceived threat and may be exacerbated if they are under the influence of substances, or because of something which happened before you visited or perhaps the person has mental ill health.

• If the person *is* under the influence of drugs or alcohol it is unlikely they are going to be able to think rationally and therefore very little is likely to be achieved. In these cases it is better to retreat early and safely. You will, of course, have to make an assessment of the safety of any children who may be in the house at the time and act on that according to your employer's guidelines. If you are feeling unsafe, it is likely the children will be too.

- Keep calm and show this by keeping your voice moderate in tone. Don't get into an argument.

- Make yourself as physically unthreatening as possible (if you are tall/big, keep a suitable distance from the agitated person). Keep as still as you can; don't make sudden or threatening movements; be aware of your facial expression and try and look as neutral as possible. Don't show that you are afraid or irritated.

- Use reflective listening but also try to reflect back the emotion. The latter requires careful judgement. If used too soon it can inflame the situation, especially if the person really just needs you to listen. However, at the right moment – generally when they are running out of steam – it can defuse the situation.

- You may choose to set a boundary: 'It isn't acceptable for you to swear at me.' If in an office (and therefore arguably safer than in a home) you may also think of setting a consequence: 'If you continue, I will leave.' The reason it may not be wise to use it in someone's home is obviously because they may very well try to block your exit. You may add, 'Would you like to have five minutes out and then we can start again?'

- If the anger appears to be about perceived past wrongs from previous experiences with authority, you may say, 'I can hear how painful an experience that was for you. I am glad you have told me because it helps me to understand how you might be feeling about us working together...[pause]...but I hope you can try and work with me. I am really looking forward to working with you.'

- If the anger is about a mistake you have made, then apologise.

- At the next appointment you have with the client you may want to reflect on what happened and think about how you might deal with conflict in the future. Sometimes people are unaware of the impact they have on you and are shocked to hear that you considered their behaviour to be threatening. If they have grown up and learnt to survive in an environment where shouting and/

or aggression is part of daily life they may be comfortable with this kind of behaviour. At best it can mean they are unaware of the impact on others but it can also be the case that they are deliberately leading you into a confrontational dialogue because it is their comfort zone. If you think this is what is happening try and explore this with your client. Do it gently and don't push as this may be covering a lot of pain and past trauma. Sometimes it's enough just to suggest this may be happening. Pause if there is no response, then try something like, 'But you know best. I'll let you have a think about it.' You can revisit it at the next appointment: 'Did you have any thoughts on…?'

- Further to this point, when an outburst is over, or at the next appointment, acknowledge the honesty in anger. Give the person permission to be angry, but not threatening. Perhaps give a concrete example: 'It was acceptable to tell me how angry you are, but not acceptable to threaten me with violence.' If appropriate, you may also want to point out that it was the aggressive behaviour you did not like/accept, not the person.

- When facing someone who is shouting, try and work out what the issue is and address that. If you can't work it out, tell the client this. 'I can hear your anger but at this point I do not understand what the specific/actual problem is. Can you help me please?' This may well initially bring further frustration but can lead to a more coherent explanation you can work with.

- Try to keep yourself grounded when faced with aggression. A simple way to do this is to keep your body physically supported. Put your feet firm and flat; lean on a sofa; hold on to a wall; pay attention to your breathing. Take deep slow breaths. This just helps you to stay calm and focused and able to make safe decisions for yourself and may also help the client to calm down.

- Faced with aggressive situations you may also learn something about yourself. We are human too and also come with varying childhood experiences, especially of attachment. Aggression can bring powerful emotions and responses in us which may surprise us. This should be explored in supervision. Helen once supervised a newly qualified social worker who had not admitted to being (justifiably) scared by the partner of a young woman with a small child and so had dropped off visiting as frequently as she should have and attempted to cover this up with potentially dire consequences for the child. This situation had triggered memories for the social worker of a frightening incident in childhood and the fear response was so strong when she was about to make a visit that she let it drop from her agenda.

In another case, aggression brought out an equally aggressive verbal response from the worker which quickly escalated into confrontation. In most cases, recognising what pushes your buttons, and learning techniques to manage this will greatly improve the relationship (and your self-esteem and confidence).

- You may hear, as we have, 'I bet you haven't met anyone as bad as me before!' said in relation to their level of aggression. We tend to reply that there isn't much we haven't seen (if this is true) in a tone conveying reassurance, not a challenge, with the underlying message that we can contain heightened emotions; we are not frightened. Some clients may have experienced parents who were unable to contain their attachment demands in childhood which led to them learning to escalate their demands (to reduce their anxiety levels) by inappropriate behaviour. It can take time and practice to relearn this behaviour and we can help by talking in a measured and friendly way until the client has been able to contain their heightened emotions just enough to continue more calmly.

- Similarly, you may hear, 'It's just a job to you.' Audrey tends to reply, 'Well the Council can pay me to visit you/make an assessment/write a report, but they can't pay me to care about you and the children and whether you like it or not, I do care about you all.' 'Why?' 'Because I happen to think that you are worth caring about.' You can only say this if you really mean it, as clients can see through insincere comments and there may be occasions when their behaviour has stretched your compassion to the limit. However, most of us are in it for that very reason and it can be a powerful message. Audrey has had experiences of this sort of conversation being the start of turning a resistant relationship into a working partnership, albeit with a lot of work along the way.

Chapter 7

Using Praise

I used to say to parents all the time, 'You need to praise your children all the time, even when they do really small things that are good. Make a fuss; say "good girl"; clap your hands; smile; offer a cuddle; say "wow!"; jump up and down and say "hurray!" or give a sticker to mark good behaviour and it will increase.'

While the above was sound advice, I was naive. I thought this was easy to do and the advice was straightforward. I had no understanding of what a hard task I was asking of parents who had not received enough praise in their own childhood or had insecure attachment patterns, low self-esteem, mental ill health or addiction issues. I had no idea how alien this request was to these parents. It took me a little while to realise what was going wrong.

I recognised that like most parenting tasks the best way to teach this is to practise what you preach, in other words to model giving praise. However, I was already doing this – constantly – by noting even the smallest of positive actions from the child by giving stickers or generally praising for good behaviour and the kids loved it. They responded by increasing their good behaviour, so I wondered what was going wrong when I didn't see mums and dads doing the same.

One day I was careful to observe a parent while I praised her child. I noticed she was watching me closely and appeared unhappy, or maybe angry. So once the child was settled on an activity I sat with her and reflected back my observation being clear that I wasn't sure what the emotion was, just that it felt like strong emotion.

Gail stated simply, 'Nobody ever did that for me and why should he be made a fuss over just for picking the bricks up. It's not hard and he is supposed to do that anyway.' Her son was 2 years old.

So I had found the problem. I think there was an issue on several levels:

- Not having enough experience of appropriate praise, it is perhaps hard to value it.

- If your own needs are not being met and you feel undervalued, it's hard to find emotional energy to praise another being.

- Gail had high expectations of her 2-year-old son and limited understanding of his developmental stage.

Gail wasn't alone in struggling with this. So, what to do about it? I decided I needed to make an effort to praise parents very precisely. My worry was that it might seem patronising but my fears proved to be unfounded.

For both children and adults, praise is most effective when:

- it is deserved, not given randomly just because you haven't done it for a while

- it's specific and descriptive ('I liked the way you coped with John's tantrum. The tone of your voice was just what was needed. Well done.')

- it's timely; timing is very important with young children; praise should be given as soon as possible, even during the action which earns the praise; with older children and adults it can sometimes be more effective to wait until they have processed the event and praise is part of the reflection

- it is given in context of a relationship; praise is more meaningful when given by someone you respect/like/look up to

- it is reinforced by more than one person.

It is also worth considering the following points:

- If there is a big achievement (e.g. good school report) it may be good if this is praised verbally but also marked with a card/small gift/outing.

- It's also appropriate to talk about the feelings that praise brings. For example, 'I was so happy when I spoke to your teacher and he said you had been listening in Maths today. I was really proud of you. Well done.'

- Exaggerate facial expressions, voice tone and action. For people who have damaged attachments, the more senses that we touch, the more able they will be to hear what we are saying.

- Practise praise on yourself. Recognise the value of your own achievements and this will help you to see the achievements of others.

People, and especially children, like tangible items to represent praise. There is something about being able to touch and hold something. It helps people to revisit the positive things that were said: 'I got that when I did well in Maths.' Or from the worker: 'I see you've still got the eraser I gave you when you did well at playtime.'

Some of the things I have given:

- a picture I have drawn

- a card

- a handmade certificate

- a key ring

- a packet of seeds to grow

- an envelope full of gold stars

- a cake I have baked

- a badge, sticker and other small gift.

I have also taken a child for an ice-cream and taken their photo.

An observation

On one occasion recently I had a student with me on a home visit. During the visit I gave both the children and the parent a lot of praise. After the visit I was reviewing what had happened with the student social worker, who challenged me, 'Don't you think it was patronising to praise the parent so much?'

I responded, 'Hmm, could be. But did you notice how Mum responded to my praise?'

My student considered this for a moment and then reflected back that Mum had responded by smiling and increasing her efforts (we were making soup) and also by praising her children. The student noted that she even sometimes used the same language as I had and concluded that I had given Mum 'what she needs' and in turn this had supported her parenting.

Chapter 8

Getting Started

We recognise that it can be daunting to try using activities with children and their families if you have not worked this way before. We don't all come into the work with lots of experience of working closely with children, but we have always believed that this is a skill that can be learned and that fun can be had along the way. In our first book *Direct Work with Vulnerable Children*[1] we gave practical advice on how to do this. Here, we asked two colleagues of Audrey's if they would tell us how and why they changed their way of working to using more activity-based methods.

Kerri's story

Kerri Meleady is a social worker in a very busy children and families team in Edinburgh. She told me that when she trained as a social worker she imagined she would be spending the best part of her days in one-to-one work with children and their families. Instead she found the volume of desk work increased over the years, so she seemed to be spending more time attending to paperwork than directly with families.

It was a particularly worrying case which brought about a change in her approach. She was working with a family of five children (from toddler to early adolescent) and their parents who had mental health and alcohol misuse problems. Kerri and a family worker had been visiting the home regularly because of concerns that all was not well, but collecting evidence of what was really happening in the home was proving difficult. As concerns grew they stepped up the visiting

---

1   Tait, A. and Wosu, H. (2012) *Direct Work with Vulnerable Children: Playful Activities and Strategies for Communication*. London: Jessica Kingsley Publishers.

schedule but this only made the parents more evasive. Eventually it was a member of the public who alerted police to abusive behaviour witnessed in the street and the children were removed and placed with kinship carers.

Kerri began to realise that a lot had gone on at home which she hadn't known about despite the fact they had been visiting regularly. Once the children began to feel safe and secure after being removed from the home, Kerri sensed there was a lot of emotional hurt buried inside and she wanted to find ways of helping them open up and get an understanding of what experiences they had had at home.

Kerri shared the work with another colleague who took responsibility for two of the children and Kerri worked with the toddler and two older children. Her first activity was 'Babies in Blankets' which is a fun, non-threatening activity with the added advantage of being edible after use! Through the conversation which this engendered, Kerri discovered they had been in overcrowded sleeping conditions; Mum would disappear for several nights at a time and Dad's mental health problems were more severe than realised.

The oldest child responded well to the activities and was ready and needed to talk about home life so Kerri spent time on one-to-one nurturing sessions (e.g. painting nails) where the young person would talk freely. Kerri's main worry was the middle child who presented as very angry and would storm out of the room, head down. Taking Audrey's advice, she went for an activity that was more fun-based. This did produce some response but she felt there was still 'a massive wall of resistance'. The child was very sensitive to any direct questions, seeing them as 'asking questions about Mum' and Kerri didn't want to put any of the children under pressure to speak badly of their parents.

Recognising the child's acute anxiety which was manifesting in anger and resistance, Kerri then modified the 'Whose job?' activity[2] by getting the child to reply to the questions by using handsignals like 'thumbs up' and 'thumbs down' and a 'not sure' finger wiggle instead of requiring the child to speak. During this game, the child

2   The 'Whose job?' activity is in Direct Work with Vulnerable Children. It is a non-threatening activity that requires children to attribute family tasks to the family members who do them.

broke down and cried and was able to say that he loved Mum but was very angry at her behaviour. She had been unable to protect the children and was often absent from the home. This was the start of the child being able to open up about his mixed feelings of love, anger and fear as they continued to work together.

Reflections

I asked Kerri how this change in approach had impacted on her work. She said that after seven months working with the children and their kinship carers using activity-based tools there was 'a massive difference' in their presentation. She believes this way of working – away from the questions and answer style – has built up trust. Their relationship was better and therefore this made therapeutic work easier. Even the kinship carer had been able to open up about her worries for the children, which she had not been able to express before.

Kerri was honest about the fact that initially she was a bit anxious but also excited at trying something new. She had to spend more time on planning and preparation (much of it in her own time). However, her confidence has grown. She admits she was disappointed in herself that she hadn't been able to get a handle on what was going on at home for these children, although she had had a gut feeling all was not well. However, there was no strong evidence even though a number of professionals were involved with the family. All they got were 'whispers in the community' and signs such as lateness for school.

Kerri is now building up her own 'tool box'. She would love to have a place to store these at work and more suitable space to work with children, but this hasn't deterred her and she continues to be determined to find ways to reach vulnerable families by building trust and making relationships through more creative and non-threatening ways of communication.

Becky's story

Becky Dunn is also a social worker in Edinburgh who uses creative ways to work with children and their families. She has given us permission to use 'Footprint', one of the very creative activities she has developed, in this book. Becky feels she was fortunate to have had experience in residential work and volunteering with ChildLine before training as a social worker, but even so said she felt that not enough emphasis is put on building relationships with families during the academic training. Students don't have enough time working directly with children to build up the skills and 'if you don't feel skilled then it is too easy to say you don't have time to work this way'. Becky has learnt, sometimes by trial and error, to do direct work with her clients and build up her own 'tool box'.

Becky has used many activities from our first book, *Direct Work with Vulnerable Children*. Her advice is that if you feel unsure about how the activity will be received, or lack confidence, practise it on a colleague. Also she finds that children tend to engage more readily than adults but if she joins the activity, modelling behaviour for them, then the parents are more willing to get involved.

Becky says that we tend to be our harshest critics, but working this way has helped her build both confidence and skill. If an activity is not working, then try something else. 'What is the worst that can happen?'

Chapter 9

The Bag

I carry around a great big bag full of resources. It has lots of pockets and hidey-holes. Children love it and can't wait to see what's in the bag and mums and dads are often interested too. Using the bag to carry my resources makes it very easy to begin a session with a positive vibe, building on the curiosity it provokes and the sense of fun. It becomes part of the routine: 'What has Audrey got in her bag?' 'What are we doing today?' I keep stickers in one pocket and snacks and drinks in another. The children very quickly learn where these pockets are. This is a great chance for me to demonstrate (or model) to mums and dads how to exercise gentle control because the children are not allowed into those pockets.

Since I started training, people often ask me about the bag I use. I tell them I tried quite a few before I found this one. You need something strong because when you haul it up and down those stairways you don't want it spilling its contents everywhere. It also has to be washable and colourful and attractive. A tall order, but I have found one and my large Tiggy bag has done great service and is much admired.[1]

---

1 Large Tiggy bags can be ordered from Skye Batiks at www.skyebatiks.com.

Chapter 10

Activities to Support Engagement

1. Babies in Blankets

This idea came from Joyce Holden, a foster carer.

Purpose

- To open up conversation about bedtimes.
- To develop or support social skills.
- To assess parent/child relationships or family dynamics.

What you need

- Jelly babies.
- Rectangular plain biscuits.
- A selection of sweets and biscuits.
- Easy roll icing.
- Tubes of coloured icing for piping.
- Small (mini) marshmallows.
- Small icing decorations (optional).
- Tin foil tray.
- Table for working on.

What to do

Place everything out on the table, getting everyone to help. Spread the items out, to encourage people to ask each other to pass things and to share. (This should give you good observational evidence on relationships and developmental stages.)

Next, demonstrate how to make a baby in a bed:

1. Take a rectangular biscuit and place it in front of you. This is the bed.

2. Place a jelly baby on top of the biscuit.

3. Using a mini marshmallow or piece of icing give your baby a pillow. Then roll out a piece of icing to make a blanket to cover the bed.

4. Place all into a small tin foil tray which represents the bedroom. Now you have your baby in a blanket.

5. Encourage creativity to decorate the room with the remaining sweets. Given a free rein you will be surprised by what they come up with.

Practice example

Emma (4) and Jane (7) had moved house three times in the past year with their mother who was fleeing domestic violence. Unsurprisingly the girls were unsettled at night and Mum found bedtimes very stressful after a long day. Everyone was tired and it would become very fraught. When Mum tried to talk about bedtime with the children they would put their hands over their ears and sing.

Mum needed help to bring routine to bedtime and also to talk about any worries or fears the girls were harbouring. Whilst the key decisions about bedtime are made by the adult, it can help to include the children in the small but important decisions like how many soft toys are allowed in the bed or how many night-time stories and who reads them.

This activity was presented to the girls and they quickly began to enjoy themselves. After about 15 minutes of exploring all the materials and learning how to make the babies in blankets, Jane began to talk spontaneously about all the different beds she had slept in. This led to conversation about which bed was best and why. She liked her 'old bed in my old house' and further conversation revealed that she was missing Dad. She also said that she liked her old room because it had 'a wee pink light and it always worked'. We made one with marshmallows for our play and Mum said she would buy a new one for her. Emma was then able to say that she didn't like sleeping in her own room as it was scary. The girls had always shared a bedroom up to now so it was agreed that they would share again for the time being.

While there was still work to be done, there was a marked improvement at bedtime. This activity allowed us to discuss it in a relaxed way, and Mum was able to show she had heard them by making small changes to make bedtimes easier for them.

II. Talking Sticks

Purpose

- To help to teach family members to take turns in conversation. This is especially helpful when you feel some members are unable to get their views heard.

What you need

- A nicely shaped stick.
- Some coloured embroidery thread.
- Feathers (packs are sold in craft stores).
- Beads or buttons.

What to do

1. Explain to the family that 'what everyone says is important' and you want to hear from everyone but you know it is sometimes hard to sit and wait your turn. Say something like:

   'So we are going to make a Talking Stick. The person who is holding the stick can speak and everyone else keeps quiet. Everybody will get a turn to hold the stick. I've got a pretty ordinary stick here but I bet we can make it more interesting. The rule is we all get to choose something to add to the stick to make it your very own talking stick. Let's start with these coloured threads. Choose your favourite colour.'

2. Show how to apply glue (or do it yourself) to the stick and wind the thread around it, leaving a long end dangling (see Figure 10.1 below).

3. Next everyone gets to choose their favourite decoration from the box and attach it to the end of their string.

4. Now you have the Talking Stick. At first you will have to help people to remember to use it. Don't get too serious. It should be fun. Try talking about something positive at first like the family dog or a TV programme. Avoid the contentious or anything too personal.

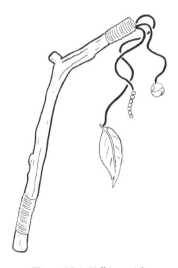

Figure 10.1: Talking stick

5. Often the adults struggle a bit more than the kids but once everyone is into the swing of it and has had a turn, stop and move to another activity or end the visit. Take the stick with you as the family is still learning to use it and until it is accepted as an essential aid in the family it could easily get lost/broken etc.

6. On the next visit, produce the stick with a flourish. This time use the stick right from the start of any discussion. At the end,

present the stick to the family, asking a parent to take charge of it and produce it when it is family talk time.

7. It can also be used on a one-to-one basis. I have a parent who uses it each time she sits down with her teenage daughter because these discussions usually get very heated. I also know a foster carer who made a miniature Talking Stick to take on bus journeys as this is when the 10-year-old twins get bored and start to argue.

III. Compliment Cards
Purpose

- To encourage family members to recognise the good things about each other and be able to tell them, with the aim of strengthening family relationships.

- To create an opportunity to help build individual self-esteem.

- To help you give the family the message that you believe they do have strengths and deserve respect even when there are serious issues to address. There are often feelings of shame, guilt, worthlessness and fear of being judged negatively. Without condoning the behaviour which brought them to the notice of social services, it is possible to build a therapeutic working relationship and, it is hoped, positive change.

What you need

- A set of compliment cards. These can be bought but they are cheaper to make.[1] Think of lots of strengths and positive attributes people have. Type them out on A4 paper and cover with laminating paper (the stuff for covering books is good and can be bought in rolls in craft shops) before cutting them out. To help you we have made a list of suggested words/ phrases in Appendix I but if you let your mind run free you will think many others.

---

1   If you want pre-printed cards a useful resource is: *Strength cards for kids,* St Luke's Innovative Resources, 137 McCrae Street, Bendigo, Victoria 3550 Australia ISBN 9781920945381, available from www.baaf.org.uk/bookshop/strength-cards-kids.

- A sheet of star stickers (optional – see 'Surprise Star Round' below).

- A quiet space.

- Enthusiasm and a sense of fun.

What to do
I have found two ways to use these with family groups and you might find many more.

Option 1
Place the cards in the middle of the table where the family is sitting. The first person lifts a card and reads it out and gives it to the person to whom they feel it is most appropriate. If they think the card applies best to themselves then they can keep it and not give it away. Move around the table with everyone taking a turn. It is helpful to have duplicates of cards so that more than one person can be 'artistic' or 'a good friend'. The facilitator (you) should also take a turn and be aware of any family member who seems to be left out or not recognised. If that does happen the facilitator needs to gently challenge this, pointing out the child's strengths. You can do this by introducing a Surprise Star Round. This is the privilege of the facilitator.

SURPRISE STAR ROUND
As the facilitator, explain to the family that you can call at any time a 'Surprise Star Round'. Invite them to take a few minutes before you begin to think about a compliment they would give each person if called upon to do so in the Surprise Star Round. If you are working with people who have memory problems or need time to process language they may want to write their ideas down to have to hand. The facilitator names the person who is to be the star. 'My star is John and I award you a star for being very good at…'.

Each family member then has the opportunity to give John a compliment. John receives a star sticker; this helps as it brings positive focus to someone who perhaps is left out. Some may find this too much attention. If that happens or you know in advance this may be a problem, you could pass round an envelope marked with their name on so they can receive their compliments without being centre stage.

Option 2

Leave the pack of compliment cards with the family for a few minutes while you find something else to do (you may be fixing a snack break). Ask them to look through all the cards and pick out the ones that best describe them as a family. On your return invite them to present them to you. You can make it fun by asking the children to do a star jump into the middle of the room and announce: 'Our family is a…family.'

You could think of other ways they could announce each card. Not all children or families will be confident enough to do this so you could add to the fun by giving a high five or clapping.

Encourage the family to give you an example of something they do that made them choose the card, keeping the tone positive and upbeat.

The next time I meet the family I will have photocopied and laminated the cards they chose for themselves and put them together by punching a hole in each card and tying them together with a ribbon to make a book. I will present this to them on my next visit with much fuss telling them it is their family strengths book. I have always had very positive responses when I have done this. A health visitor once said to me that on one of her visits to the family the mother showed her the book which I had made for them saying, 'so it is not all bad'. This was a family with children registered under child protection procedures and there had been strong resistance to engaging with social workers.

Practice example

Aidan (8) and his father were from the Travelling community. They lived in a high- rise block of flats in a social housing scheme. The father, Larry, had mental health problems. Aidan was not attending school and there were concerns about his social and emotional needs being met. Larry's physical care of Aidan was good and other relatives would visit to ensure he was being fed and there was heating etc. In the summer months Aidan would go on the road with them, leaving Dad behind. In the initial weeks since referral Larry had been difficult to engage. I had eventually gained entry by building rapport by telling a Scottish folk story through the letterbox. The following two visits were spent exchanging stories with each other. On the second one I told a story about a boy called Aidan who lived with his dad, Larry, and they had a social worker called Audrey. It was clear that the family had developed a deep distrust of social workers and I was determined to change that perception. On the third visit I used strength cards. Larry and Aidan worked together to show me their family strengths. I used Option 2, and had added new cards that I thought would be particularly relevant like 'storytelling', 'driving', 'building things' etc. They were enthusiastic and I made lots of fuss both about their identified strengths but also about the process and how well they worked together. This led us to acknowledge Aidan's role in caring for Larry and the role the wider family had in helping Larry with Aidan's care.

At the next appointment Aidan was out playing but I presented Larry with the strengths book. He smiled briefly and put it aside saying, 'I've no time for that nonsense' to which I smiled and said with humour, 'Oh, it's nonsense indeed. You can't fool me, and Aidan will like it.' To this Larry nodded and said 'You're not as green as you are cabbage-looking' (a Scots saying which means you are wiser than you look) to which I laughed. We had established rapport.

For me the obvious presenting issue was Aidan's non-attendance at school and Larry's mental health. However, that was my agenda and I was pretty sure it wasn't Larry's or Aidan's. There are times when it is important to put your agenda temporarily aside and start with the client's. This shifts the balance of power and encourages partnership working. So I asked Larry how I could help him. His reply was brief and to the point:

'You can't help me unless you just get out of my life.'

'I'm afraid that's not going to happen and I think you know that. Besides, I like you and Aidan, so you are stuck with me. Come on, let's think: if there was something you would like to change what would it be?'

Larry replied, 'Nowt I want to change.'

'Okay, fair enough. Let me have a look at that strengths book and see what things this family is good at.' I flicked through the book acknowledging all the strengths and then handed it to Larry, 'Which one is the most important one to you?'

Larry looked briefly at the book, 'Ach, there's not much important here.'

I resisted objecting to this, instead reflecting back his statement which gave me a bit of thinking time.

'You are telling me there is nothing of importance in the strengths book?'

'Aye.'

'Okay, so what is important to you? What did we miss?'

'Well, I always make sure the lad is clean and fed and got everything he needs.'

'Sure, that is important. You are telling me that Aidan's physical care is important and you do it well. I would agree with that. But you know that we can all do better. What would you like to do, or what do you need that would improve Aidan's care?'

'He needs a new bed. That one through there is on its last legs and I can't afford a new one.'

I checked the bed. It was in a bad state and had been repaired several times and the mattress was mouldy.

'Okay, would you accept a new bed if I got one?'

He agreed and the next week a bed was delivered from a local charity. I then went back to the strengths book. 'So what is next? What are we going to make even better?'

Aidan picked out the 'you are a good friend' card and said he wanted to go to school because he wanted to be a good friend to more people.

I was secretly delighted he had picked out something from my agenda. Larry had a lot of objections. There was no need to go to school; he had no uniform and so on. Both Aidan and I worked as a team to find some solutions. Aidan's motivation was to spend more time with the children in the community. He wasn't highly motivated to learn, saying he could write his name and read a little and that was enough. I accepted that but said if he went to school part of being a good friend is to do what your friends do and share good times and bad times. Aidan and Larry agreed.

So Aidan began to attend school occasionally and that was fine for a start. His attendance was running at 20 per cent. (Two years later it had improved to 79%).

We continued to work with the strengths book and added to it. I noted that Larry always knew where it was – never far from where he could reach it. When we had built up some trust I was able to introduce a Community Psychiatric Nurse (CPN) to Larry and he now takes medication which has stabilised his mood and makes him more able to be emotionally available to Aidan. Eventually he was able to admit he was struggling to care for Aidan and that the family supports were not as strong as he had first made out. Aidan now has respite care once a month with a foster carer. Work with this family has extended to long term and it has been a privilege to see all their strengths grow. Others have been added. For Larry, 'working with Audrey and the CPN' and 'being able to say when I need help'. For Aidan, 'going to school to learn and be a friend' and 'going to stay with another family sometimes so I can teach them stories and learn how they live'.

IV. Fruit Sculptures
Purpose

- To promote conversation, sharing, healthy eating, education about fruit and to have fun. This is also a good relationship-building activity.

- To give an opportunity to assess family dynamics, parenting capacity, speech and language, social and motor skills and self-esteem.

- To provide an opportunity for the worker to provide praise and encouragement to raise self-esteem whilst modelling parenting skills.

- To encourage the family to try new tasks.

- To provide a fun, easy and relatively cheap activity that parents can try again with their children.

What you need

- Cocktail sticks.

- An assortment of fruit. As the aim is to make funny faces with fruit, bring a selection of different sized fruit which can be used for the eyes, nose etc. For example:

  - apples

  - oranges

  - bananas

  - grapes

  - blueberries

  - raisins

  - strawberries

  - any other fruit which is local to you.

- I also carry with me a small fold-up table as I have found many families I work with don't have a table.

- It's also a good idea to encourage everyone to wash their hands before handling (and eating) the fruit.

What to do

This activity can last 10 minutes or an hour depending on the level of enthusiasm, concentration and amount of fruit available.

1. Set all the fruit out on the table, naming it and talking with the children as you do this.

2. Give each child some cocktail sticks. Show them they are sharp and tell them they are being trusted to be careful.

3. Invite the children to choose their first piece of fruit. Start with the larger, firmer fruit to build the face on, for example an apple, orange or banana.

4. Show them how to put a cocktail stick into another piece of fruit and pin it onto the 'face' to represent an eye, nose etc.

5. Once you have done this the children will usually become very creative and enthusiastic and your focus can then be on offering praise and encouragement, modelling good parenting and taking the opportunity to observe.

Practice example

This is a family I was visiting for the first time after the five children were registered to be monitored under child protection procedures. Their mother, a single parent, was angry, upset and resistant to having a social worker. It was critical I get over the doorstep, try to establish rapport and begin to get to know them in order to make a proper assessment and plan work with the family.

I chose this activity because I thought it would span the age group and I already knew the children liked fruit as they had enjoyed oranges and grapes from my bag on the previous visit. I also wanted to be as unthreatening as possible and for the whole family to get something from the visit. I knew if they had fun it would open the door to further visits when the hard work had to be done. In addition I felt Mum might appreciate having the fruit to give to the children as I knew she had limited funds.

I arrived at the door with a bag of fruit and a small fold-up table. My aim was to be fun and friendly but ready to be firm and insistent on entry if necessary. Mum opened the door with the youngest children behind her and a sullen teenager in the background. She didn't invite me in so I held up my bag and, addressing the children as brightly as possible, told them I had a really fun thing to do and asked who wanted to see what was in the bag. There was a flurry of interest which prompted me to say, 'I have to come in first' and I looked at Mum for permission, which she grudgingly gave. The teenager picked up the table and offered to help put it up. I was in.

The table was quickly set up and the children gathered around it. Making eye contact with the mother I told her it was good to see her again and thanked her for inviting me in. I asked if she would like to join the activity or go and make herself a cup of tea and put her feet up while I entertained the children. She readily took the second option, saying she was exhausted.

I sat down with the children and showed them the activity. As expected they were full of enthusiasm and fun and we had lively conversation including swear words, which I advised were not okay (I was establishing boundaries here). They were finding it hard to share but I had enough fruit so they didn't have to fight over it. I began to praise each child's efforts and encourage them to admire each other's work. I gave the teenager her place as my helper and was careful to address her according to her age, whilst at the same time encouraging her to have fun with the younger children. The tone of the session was deliberately light with as much fun and laughter as possible.

Mum wandered in with her cup of tea and we showed her the sculptures. I was able to compliment her on the children, giving specific praise. Kevin had very creative ideas; Amy was very caring and helpful and so on.

My hour was nearly up so I gave the five-minute warning for tidying up. Giving Mum some food wrap, I suggested some of the children might like to take a sculpture to school to show the teacher and their friends in the hope this might attract some positive attention and the opportunity to feel special. I thanked her for having me and suggested we make another appointment during the week when the children were in school, so we could talk. She agreed.

As I left I knew I had the beginnings of an assessment of the individual children and family dynamics. I had begun to establish rapport, established boundaries, respect and co-operation and believed we were on the way to establishing a good working relationship.

V. Baking and Cooking
Purpose

- To promote conversation and to have fun. This is also a good relationship-building activity.

- To assess family dynamics.

- To provide praise and encouragement to raise self-esteem whilst modelling parenting skills.

- To encourage the family to improve their diet by home cooking.

- To provide a fun, easy and relatively cheap way activity that parents can try again with their children.

What you need

- The worker may need to provide some basic cooking or baking tools and equipment.

Practice example

Carly was approaching her 15th birthday. She had had a very difficult start in life witnessing domestic violence and being parented by a mother who was using drugs. I hadn't known her then but we often talked about her experiences as they had a huge impact on how she presented now. Her relationship with her mother (Dawn) was poor, with frequent volatile arguments, and now Carly was about to become a big sister and was not too happy about it. She felt she was enough for her mother. Why did she want a baby anyway, and more critically, did this mean that the father of the baby, who Carly didn't like, would be in their lives forever?

Mum was confused by Carly's anger. She felt she was doing fine. She was drug free, in a stable relationship with a man who was not abusive and had thought that Carly would be as delighted as she was. Mother and daughter were gradually disengaging. Both were hurt and angry. It was very raw and neither felt able to meet to try and talk things through. I needed an activity that would be non-threatening, enjoyable and would require them both to work together.

On one visit Mum complained that she was struggling financially. She further complained that each week she bought Carly chocolate but this week Carly had eaten it all at once and was demanding more. Mum explained that it was expensive, but to keep the peace she had given in and bought more. As a result she was short on money to put in the electricity meter in the home. I decided that next visit I would make Chocolate Biscuit Cake with Carly and her mum. I explained to Mum that it would be cheaper than buying sweeties. Mum didn't cook or bake but was interested in learning and Carly liked chocolate so both agreed to the activity.

The next week I bought the ingredients and went to meet them the day before Mum did her weekly shop. I wanted to make the cake before then, to give mum the opportunity to say 'no' to Carly's requests for sweets whilst at the same time ensuring Carly did get a sweet treat in the form of a cake. Carly and Mum had had a difficult weekend. At the start of the visit they were not talking to each other and were both anxious to tell me their version of events. I refused to allow them to do this and stated firmly that we were going to make the cake. This was to try to avoid an argument which could potentially have led to one or the other storming out. The purpose of this visit was to try to improve the relationship and I knew that I could return to discuss the difficulties later.

Despite some reluctance from both parties, I carried on as if nothing was amiss in a bright and cheery manner. I got them organised in the kitchen and gave directions to each one as to what I wanted them to do. I made sure they had to work together and help each other and made a big point of frequently adding 'please' and 'thank you' to my instructions. This prompted Carly to say 'thank you' to her mum when she passed the bowl and I then whispered in Mum's ear to say 'thank you' to Carly. My purpose was to begin respectful verbal communication as they were still glowering at each other.

My next strategy was to compliment their team work, minimal as it was. Positive expectations which are verbalised can bring surprisingly big results.

'You guys are working well together.'

'That was great team work.'

'Carly, I liked the way you helped Mum hold the bowl. Nice work.'

'Mum, that was lovely of you to help Carly there.' She had moved a spoon out of the way. I was commenting on even the smallest positive action and before long I had two smiling people who were relaxing.

So then I tried to get them to compliment each other.

'Dawn, you must be so proud of your daughter. Carly is such a nice young woman and quick to learn how to bake. She's a real credit to you.'

'Aye. She's no bad. She has her moments,' replied Dawn.

Then a little later, 'Carly, isn't it nice that your mum is letting us use her kitchen and it's lovely that she is joining in.'

'Aye, it's good.'

By now the cake was in the tin and ready to be put in the refrigerator to set. This whole process took about 25 minutes. I then wanted to use the time while we were waiting for the cake to set to discuss the weekend. We chatted about baking and cooking for a few minutes and then very calmly I said, 'So tell me about your weekend.'

Dawn was still quite calm when she told me about her daughter's behaviour, which although very testing for the adult, was pretty normal teenage behaviour. Carly then gave her version and was a little more animated but managed to contain her feelings well. Together we talked the issues through and I supported Dawn in her limit-setting and we negotiated a sanction that left Carly rather sullen, as she was losing her pocket money. She was about to stomp off when I used the well-used distraction technique of announcing brightly, 'Goodness I forgot about the cake. It must be ready. Come on, Carly, we'd better get it out of the fridge.'

The distraction worked and we all moved to the kitchen. Carly was given the responsibility to remove the cake and start the next stage.

A word here about understanding and managing a situation like this which is very common when working with teenagers: Carly is a young person with low self-esteem and so her resilience and ability to cope with arguments and sanctions is limited. She, like other children in her position, tends to internalise an argument and interpret it as meaning that she is bad or not loved and then act defensively, either withdrawing or presenting challenging behaviour. This can result in more arguments over the presenting behaviour which very quickly becomes a circular pattern for both parties. If this pattern is not broken, eventually it can lead to a relationship breakdown.

Back in the kitchen, I got them working together to spread the chocolate on top of the cake and decorate it, reinforcing the relationship. This whole process had taken approximately 75 minutes. At this point I left the house to let them do this together, giving them the opportunity to have a positive experience without me there. I told them I would call later to see if they liked the cake, thereby offering continuity of care – a transition from doing the activity with me to doing part of it on their own with me checking in. I called later as promised. Carly was out but Dawn told me the cake was great – so good that Carly was out selling it to neighbours, so she could make money to buy sweets. Very enterprising.

The following week we made soup. I followed the same pattern of engagement, which is to:

- organise people in the kitchen

- give instructions in such a way that people have to work together or help each other

- compliment their team work

- create opportunities for them to compliment each other

- while the soup is cooking, have a discussion about the previous week and address any issues

- use distraction if needed by focusing on the progress of the soup

- leave before the soup is ready and call back later.

Soup has the added benefit of improving the family's diet. Neither Dawn nor Carly had made soup before and this was a good way to use her fruit and vegetable vouchers.[2] The following week we made a different soup recipe; the following week, scones and after that a sponge cake, each time using the same routine as above. The first two weeks I provided the ingredients but then I asked Dawn to buy them, which she did.

Also the first week I brought all the baking utensils we needed including bowls, spoons and baking tins. I only produced them after I had checked with them, 'Do you have a mixing bowl? A pan?' etc. and if the answer was negative I would rummage in my bag saying, 'Hang on a minute, I may have something here.' Not everyone has these things and I wanted to cause minimal embarrassment for the family and also find out what they needed and then get some of these items from charity shops. I also encouraged Dawn and Carly to save up for items like weighing scales and cake tins.

I find that starting with making a cake is more attractive for families and hooks them in, before we move to more healthy food. It is not uncommon for me to work with families who have never made a pot of soup or a baked potato. A lot of the families I work with survive on ready-made meals, sometimes because they have never been shown how to cook and sometimes as they are perceived as being cheaper. For example, one parent I worked with told me she could buy five meals for £5. This was easy to calculate but not as cheap as cooking for yourself. I try to find out their favourite ready-made meal and then teach them how to make that. Macaroni cheese and shepherd's pie are favourites.

A year on, Carly continues to make her Chocolate Biscuit Cake[3] and sell it and I had a lovely surprise when I made a home visit and a very excited Dawn rushed me through to the kitchen to show me the soup she had made. She very proudly announced that her baby, now at the weaning stage, also loved it.

---

2   Discounted vouchers available to some communities in Edinburgh to be spent on vegetables.
3   See Appendix II for the recipe.

Activities to Aid Assessment and/ or Help With 'Big Conversations'

1. Dream Houses
Purpose

- This is a fun activity that brings everyone in the family together. The aim is to help build rapport and give the worker the opportunity to start assessing family dynamics. It will help assess child development and parenting skills. It also gives the family an opening to talk about personal experiences in a non-threatening way.

What you need

- A3 paper – enough for everyone plus a few spare sheets.

- Felt tip pens in different tip widths from fine to broad, in as many different colours as you can find. It is always worth investing in good quality pens. Check they are all still functioning properly.

- A table. You can work on the floor if there is no table.

What to do

1. Gather everyone around the table or in a circle on the floor and show them the pens, pointing out the different tip widths and colours. Then have a discussion about homes in general. Flats,

apartments, houses, castles, Hobbit holes, fairy doors in trees and so on.

2. Give everyone a piece of paper and ask them to draw you their dream house. What would it be like? Would it be magic? Would it have doors and do they lock? Would it have wheels and if so where would you travel to? How would you make it special just for you? How would you make it safe?

3. Once the houses have been drawn, ask them to show each other and talk about all the special features.

Practice example

This was a family of four children aged from 4 years to 14 years. Laura was the mother of all the children and Bernard was the stepfather. The two oldest children had been sexually abused by their birth father who used to live with them. The family had moved six times in the past year.

The presenting problem was that Tilly (13) and Tom (11) were having difficulties in school. In addition, Alexandra (8) said she didn't like her new house and was having difficulty sleeping. I invited the family to the office to do this activity as there was a big table there and no distractions.

The activity resulted in lots of conversations around house moves and good and bad parts of each of the family homes. It also led to discussion about money, as Laura showed her dream home.

Tom started to talk about safety features and his ability to deal with anger. Tilly talked about ways she would stop people entering her bedroom. In later sessions with Tilly on her own, the picture of her dream house allowed me to enter into a conversation about the abuse she had experienced.

Laura and Bernard had much strength as parents but family life was busy and the dynamics of the reconstructed family proved challenging. Sometimes it was hard to make space to deal with the difficult stuff. The family continued to engage in work with me over a number of months. They reported that having set time to come to the office and do this kind of work on a regular basis really helped. It created opportunities for problems to be addressed regularly so they didn't become unmanageable. The family is now functioning independently of social work support but report they still sometimes have 'family table time' where they do some of the activities we did together by themselves while they address issues which arise in family life.

Figure 11.1: Dream House drawn by child

'There are big dogs in the garden so no one gets past without them growling and biting. There are look-out towers so I know who is coming and a boxing ring and punch bag to help me with my anger. And a big strong door only dad and I can open.'

II. Family Drawing
Purpose

- This is an activity that everyone in the family can do together, regardless of age or stage of development. Children enjoy the shared experience of playing with the parent(s), in some families a rare event.

- It provides an excellent opportunity for assessment of family dynamics and parenting skills and also an opportunity to work on these.

- The activity taps into childhood but is not perceived as 'play', which some parents find difficult to do.

- At the end of the activity, the family have produced a piece of artwork that they can all claim. As a worker you can make this time special to increase the sense of belonging and pride in achievement.

- It is often experienced as a relaxing fun activity and it is something a parent can do with children later. It is affordable and easy to set up.

What you need

- A table and chairs. (I have a camping table in my car as not infrequently I work with families who don't have a table. This activity can be done on the floor, but in general, children settle better at a table.)

- A large piece of paper. I often use flipchart paper or wallpaper lining.

- A choice of plenty of crayons, pens and pencils in working order.

- Sticky tape.

What to do

1. Stick the paper to the table with sticky tape.

2. Make sure everyone can reach the crayons etc.

3. Invite everyone to draw on the paper. I usually start with 'anything you like' but sometimes older children and adults struggle to get started so if that happens I might say, 'Let's all draw circles and see what we can make them into.' Circles easily become balloons, wheels, lollipops and so on. If someone is still struggling, invite them to draw a circle and colour it in, so that they are part of the activity.

4. Once the paper is full, especially if this happens quickly as it usually does, offer another piece.

Family portrait option

One option is to ask the people to do a family portrait, either drawing themselves or agreeing who will draw whom. This can be a useful exercise in directed work as it usually leads to conversations about each family member. However, in my experience it is better to know your family quite well before doing this. Often remarks can be personal or family members can use this activity to have a go at each other so you need to be in a position where you have their trust and respect so you can intervene to keep everyone emotionally safe.

At the end of the activity, identify somewhere you can hang the picture. I like to take a photo and put this in a simple clip frame. It is a good gift to give at the end of your work together. It then becomes a special item.

Simple as it is, this activity again and again proves to be popular with families and provides me a lot of scope for assessment of family dynamics, parenting skills and child development. If you can, leave paper and crayons with the family. They are more likely to do it again if they have the tools.

Practice example

I was working with a single parent of three children, two girls of 16 years and 4 years and a boy of 18 months. The children had previously been involved in child protection procedures and were now monitored under the Scottish Children's Hearing System on a supervision order. Mum, Debbie, had been addicted to heroin and was now nearly at the end of a methadone programme. She was meeting the majority of her children's needs but struggled enormously with being consistent, especially with boundaries. In particular, she found her daughter Claire, aged 4, very challenging.

Claire was developing well and like most 4-year-olds had lots of energy and pushed the boundaries. As Debbie was often shifting the boundaries, Claire would push until she established what the boundary was at that moment, in her attempts to feel safely contained by Debbie. Mum found this exhausting and had begun to be very negative about Claire, unable to find any positives, and actually had begun to say she didn't like her very much.

Claire, like most 4-year-olds, liked to draw. The 16-year-old, Carmel, liked to colour in. Debbie, to her credit, appreciated the art work they did and displayed it in the home. I wanted to introduce an activity where Debbie could praise Claire and that everyone could do together and enjoy.

I didn't tell Debbie in advance that we were going to do a family activity as I wanted to model how to give the children a surprise which was cheap, simple and easy to do and could be done in about an hour (my limit for a home visit).

Carrying all I needed with me, including a small fold-up table, I arrived at the door and with much enthusiasm announced I had a surprise today for everyone. The girls clamoured around me and even the baby in Mum's arms picked up on the excitement and babbled and kicked his legs. Debbie was also smiling as I set up the table with the girls' help. By the time I got my art box out of the bag, all family members were engaged.

I showed the new pens I had brought with me especially for them and baby James grabbed one and started scribbling. I told them we were going to do the biggest drawing ever and that everyone was going to join in. Claire could hardly contain her excitement but Carmel was looking a bit nonplussed. Giving Debbie a pen, I quietly whispered to her that I challenged her to have fun and to give as much praise as possible to Claire. She nodded and started to draw.

Carmel then needed my attention so I asked if she wanted to work as a team with me. I got eye contact and a nod, 'but I can't draw'. I suggested I draw and she would colour in. She asked me to draw the logo of her favourite band which I did and she sat happily colouring in.

They all quickly settled into the activity and I noted that Debbie had still not praised Claire but she had given James a lot of attention and praised Carmel's work. I praised Claire and invited Debbie to join in, 'What lovely colours. What do you think, Mum?' Debbie agreed but in a very flat tone, without looking at Claire's work. I noted that Carmel had picked up on my remark and offered, 'You like pink like me, that's good, Claire!'

We continued with the activity with periods of conversation and silence. Everybody appeared to be relaxing. I offered positive comments to all four in this period and when I had the opportunity, whispered to Debbie, 'Remember our challenge.' This brought a smile and a couple of minutes later she said, 'I like your drawing, Claire,' with positive emotion and good eye contact.

This resulted in Claire hugging Mum and in doing so she bumped into James who let out a wail. Debbie began to tell Claire off and I was about to intervene when Carmel said, 'Come on, Mum, it was just an accident.' Debbie looked at me. I nodded, 'Just an accident.' Debbie responded by cuddling Claire and telling her to be more careful next time. I gave her a thumbs up. Fifteen minutes before I needed to be leaving, I modelled for Debbie how to end a play session with minimum fuss by giving a warning it was nearly time to finish and then a five-minute warning and finally said, 'tidy-up time'. I supported the tidy-up by directing and praising and this was done with minimum protest from the children.

What I hope was gained here was:

- The children had a positive family experience.

- Debbie practised recognising positive behaviour and giving praise.

- Self-esteem was supported and, I hope, raised.

- Debbie was shown an activity to help support the development of the younger children (fine motor skills; hand and eye co-ordination; literacy; encouraging imagination; social skills).

- It proved to be a good assessment opportunity.

III. Activity Menu
Purpose

- To help a family plan and negotiate activities.

- To help a child to decide how they will spend their day and develop appropriate independence.

What you need

- Cord (to hang the chart when finished).

- Pens – good quality.

- A large piece of card.

- You will also need an appropriate method of sticking the charts to the wall without damaging the surface. There are several such products on the market usually available in craft or stationery stores.

What to do

This is a very simple but effective activity.

1. Cut out 2-inch (5cm) squares of card – at least 30. You want as many as possible.

2. Invite the group individually to draw or write all the activities they can possibly think of doing. This should include mundane things that have to be done every day like eating or housework, as well as hobbies, playing with toys, games they enjoy and outings.

3. Now write at the top of the large piece of card 'AM' and half way down 'PM' For young children you could use pictures to signify the time of day and for older children the face of a clock. Whatever you choose it should be what is best for the youngest in the family group.

4. Now have a look through the pictures together and work out a 'menu' for the day. You can ask the family to show you:

   ○ an ordinary day

   ○ a special day

   ○ Dad's (or Mum's /sister's/brother's favourite day)

   ○ what they are doing tomorrow.

5. Place the chosen cards onto the 'menu' in a list as if making a timetable for the day.

This usually provokes lots of discussion between family members. You might ask them first to choose the 'have to do' cards like washing, dressing, eating. Next, the 'keeping busy cards' might include tidying up, washing up, household chores, playing, drawing, reading, listening to music or watching TV. Finally the 'nice things to do' could be going to the play-park, baking, going to a friend's house.

The process of the activity helps to develop negotiating skills, planning and problem solving as well as telling you something about how the family works.

Practice example

Jane was 12 years old with global developmental delay. She lived with foster carers and five other children. Her carer reported that Jane required a lot of support every day; she couldn't organise her day independently and required constant direction. For example she could complete a task or activity she was given but when finished would look to her foster carer for direction as to what to do next. If the carer was not near, or available, her behaviour would become demanding and disruptive. Jane had a short attention span of about 15 minutes and the carer was exhausted.

I visited Jane in school and we made activity cards and a wall chart. She was amazed at how many activities she could come up with for around the house. 'I never knew there was so much I could do. I don't remember all that!'

Initially we didn't include any activities which occurred outside the home, other than going to school. This was deliberate as the purpose was to help her to be self-reliant around the home.

Jane began to use her Activity Menu (or My Home Timetable as she liked to call it) immediately. She put it up on her bedroom wall without telling her foster carer what it was (although I had briefed her) and the carer noticed immediately that instead of going to them frequently she began to run up and down the stairs to her room. When asked what she was doing, she replied, 'Just checking what to do next.'

When I saw her the following week she told me she had been using her Home Timetable.

'I do lots of stuff now and I choose.'

'Good lass!'

'And I don't need to ask anyone no more what to do next and I think Doris [foster carer] likes that.'

'Well done. Have you shown it to Doris yet?'

'No. It's my secret 'cause I think it makes me more like the other kids.'

Doris confirmed the newfound independence. When the next school holidays came around I asked Jane if we could teach Doris how to make a chart so that everybody could be involved in choosing an activity over the holiday period. I was hoping this would help Jane feel less different as I wondered if keeping it a secret indicated she felt she was abnormal or different from the other kids.

Jane was keen to teach Doris how to make an Activity Menu and Doris responded with enthusiasm and praise. We then did a session with the whole family, breaking the holiday down into 14 days of menu charts. This was because Doris was keen to plan for the whole holiday period rather than doing it on a day-to-day basis. This was a big job and we needed loads of activity cards but the five kids and two adults got through it and when we finished, the kitchen was wallpapered with the charts.

The whole activity generated lots of excellent discussion around looking after oneself:

'Do we really need to eat three times a day?'

'Why do I have to shower every day?'

'Why can't we go to the zoo more than once?' which generated talk about managing money and taking everyone's wishes into account.

I left the family to get on with it after we had done the menu for two days. Doris phoned me after the holidays;

'See these Activity Menus,' she said, 'the best thing I have ever done. So simple and so fair. We avoided all the endless rows about what we were doing each day and the kids were so organised. They got up each day and knew what they had to do before we could go out for the day. It was just so much easier. Thank you!'

I have used these Activity Menus with a lot of families now. It has been particularly helpful for parents who have memory problems. A lot of adults who have abused drugs or alcohol have issues with organisation and memory which is sometimes misinterpreted as not caring enough for their children to do things with them. It also empowers children to have an input into family life.

For a lot of the families I work, with I need to give them extra support to help them carry out the menu plans. For example, one small girl had visited a local castle with school and she drew a picture of the castle and said she wanted to go again with her mum. Mum was adamant she couldn't do this so I used the Spider and Bird activity[1] to break down what the barriers were to making this visit and working out solutions. One was money and I was able to help through a charity fund. But far more significant was the lack of confidence, 'People like me don't go to places like that,' and 'I don't know how to get there.'

We worked out a quieter time to visit the castle and I dropped them off by car with directions how to get home. This included pointing out where to buy the tickets and waiting for them to enter and waving cheerfully.

Half an hour later I called Mum on her mobile as we agreed I would do.

'It's great. I love it!'

The next holiday period they made another visit themselves including another tourist attraction nearby. The little girl was delighted and had something to share in school about her holidays which boosted her confidence.

IV. Our Street/Our Community
Purpose

- This activity is perhaps most useful in the initial assessment stage. It allows you to find out how the family define their world.

---

1   The Spider and Bird Activity is a three-part exercise, which helps clients break down problems, which are affecting their lives, and to look for solutions. See Tait, A. and Wosu, H. (2012) *Direct Work with Vulnerable Children: Playful Activities and Strategies for Communication.* London: Jessica Kingsley Publishers.

- It frequently leads to conversations about relationships in the community and has helped me to identify wider supports I had not been previously aware of.

What you will need

- A selection of different sizes of cardboard boxes and cardboard trays (like the ones used to stack tins in supermarkets).
- Poster paints
- Glue and sticky tape.

What to do

This activity is best done over two or three sessions of 45 minutes each.

Session 1

Invite the parent(s) and child(ren) to make a replica of their street/community using the cardboard trays for a base and the boxes to create buildings. You will usually find that the children lead and the adults eventually get into the fun of it too, but you may need to help at first. 'That box looks a similar shape to your building. What do you think?'

If you are working with more than one child, put several trays together to make a bigger base. The family should define what they consider to be their street/community, which in itself will be of interest to you. For example, one family I worked with made a model that included the street they lived in and extended this to the school, park, community centre, shops and social worker centre. They considered all of these places as being their community. Another family who lived in high-rise flats considered only their own block and the neighbouring one as their community. A further family left out the opposite side of the road, as they said this was another area and they would never go there. Then I understood why, despite my best efforts, the children were not accessing the children's groups at the local community centre because although it was 'just over the road' it was in the no-go area. I was able to get them places in another centre 15 minutes further away but in 'their area' and the children began to attend the groups.

Session 2

Paint the model and add features, including a bit of texture. You can mix a little sand with the paint to create a look like bricks. Similarly, cotton wool can be made to look like grass by sticking it onto the card and painting it green. Sponges cut into small pieces and painted grey are stones or rocks. Use lollipop sticks to make benches; create some people out of play dough or plasticine. You can add toy cars and animals. The family could do some of this on their own and then when you come back you can help with the fine details.

There can be lovely conversations as you do this. One of the ones that made the biggest impression on me was with an 8-year-old girl, her older brother in his 20s (who really got into building the model accurately) and Mother. When we made people they started telling me about all the people who lived in their community; who they were and what they did; how they behaved and who to stay away from. The conversations made me aware of all the connections they had in the community and how they engaged with them and who their support systems were. We had previously thought this was a socially isolated family.

Session 3

Now that the paint is dry, play with the model!

You can help stimulate play. 'Show me how to get to the shops' or 'There was once a boy called Jack (child's name) and he lived at number 3 Cherry Tree House (the child's address). Every morning he got up to go to school, had his breakfast and then…' Pass the story to the child saying, 'You tell me what happens now as I don't know.'

You can ask Mum, Dad, brothers and sisters all to tell a story using the model. Ask them if they are going to tell a true story or a made up one.

Practice example

Eileen was 7 years old and lived with her mum who had significant mental health problems and rarely left the house. An older brother lived with them and there was an adult sister who visited regularly. Eileen enjoyed outings with her brother and sister and they supported her to keep doctor and dentist appointments, go to school events and parents' nights and so on. But what Eileen really wanted was to go out with Mum. We tried lots of ways to make this happen. I worked closely with the Community Psychiatric Nurse but despite Mum's best efforts and lots of professional support it just wasn't working and Eileen was very disappointed.

I decided to do this activity with Eileen and her mum. Eileen was very creative and her mum enjoyed playing with her. With minimal support they made a beautiful model including school, play-park, shops etc.

In Session 3 when we were playing with the model, I asked Eileen to show Mum where she would like to take her and what they would do together if her dream came true and Mum went out with her. Eileen played out Mum taking her to the shop and buying her an ice lolly and returning home. Mum was visibly moved, but said, 'I'll give you money to go and get a sweetie, dear.' Eileen's response was that her mother didn't come with her like other mums and she didn't like that.

Eileen's mum then took the dolls saying, 'My turn.' She acted out taking Eileen to the park and pushing her on the swings saying, 'That's what I would do.'

In the following weeks Eileen continued to use the model to show Mum what she did when she was outside. Mum, who was upset by her daughter's clear requests that she join her outside and Eileen's obvious disappointment and anger, was making me wonder if I had done the right thing. I had given the child a voice and the ability to express her strong feelings, but it was beginning to cause Mum distress and impact on her parenting. I began to think of how I could remove the model from the home without causing Eileen distress, ('Can I borrow it to show other people?'). However, on my next visit to Mum while Eileen was at school, I arrived to find her with her coat on. 'I've got to get myself outside for the sake of the bairn. Will you come with me to the lift just to go down and come back up again?'

So we did that. Over the next few weeks her older children took the lead in supporting her and four months later she managed to stand outside the back door of the flats and watch Eileen playing in the park.

A further eight weeks on and Mum managed to go out of the front door of the flats and buy an ice-cream from the travelling ice-cream van. Two years on and Mum can make it to school occasionally and to the shop and is able to take Eileen to the doctor.

The model is still in the family living room.

V. Bereavement Box
Purpose

- To provide an opportunity to talk about death, funerals etc. and to be able to role play using some of the items.

- To provide an opportunity to talk about memories.

What you need

- An attractive box. I used a shoe box and covered it with gold paper.

- A small doll which looks like a fairy or angel. You can customise your own.

- A star-shaped box. These can be bought from craft stores but I conveniently had an old star-shaped chocolate box. Cover in attractive paper.

- A small bag of stones:

  - a rough one

  - a smooth one

- ○ a precious one.
- A small model of a coffin made from cardboard.
- Some artificial flowers.
- A small porcelain jar.
- A candle.
- Pictures of grave stones cut out and laminated.
- Pictures of different religious symbols or buildings (optional).
- An owl puppet.
- A story book about bereavement, for example, *Badger's Parting Gifts* by Susan Varley, *Water Bugs and Dragonflies* by Doris Stickney, *What on Earth Do You Do When Someone Dies?* by Trevor Romain.[2]
- A rainbow. I have a wooden one but you could make one out of clay or cardboard.
- A box of tissues.

Place all of the above in the box to make your own Bereavement Box.

What to do

I keep this box in a big cloth bag along with other activities for children to choose. When I first visit children, generally I explain all the activities/toys in my bag and they can decide what they want to play with. The contents of my bag change but a few items are always there – felt tip pens; rabbit puppet; play dough; games and the Bereavement Box.

Children are naturally curious about what is in the box so most of them have a quick look and some want to use it immediately. Others reject it and never look at it again. Others explore it and then put it back and go back to it when they are ready to talk about it. Some children take certain items out of the box and leave others inside. All

2   Varley, S. (2013) *Badger's Parting Gifts.* London: Andersen Press; Stickney, D. (1982,1997) *Water Bugs and Dragonflies.* Cleveland, OH: The Pilgrim Press; and Roman, T. (1999) *What on Earth Do You Do When Someone Dies?* Minneapolis, MN: Free Spirit Publishing.

of this is good and safe because it is child-led. They choose and they dictate the pace.

This box should be available to all children even if they have not experienced a bereavement or loss yet. It serves the purpose of demystifying death and therefore reducing the secrecy that surrounds it. There is comfort in knowing it is there if they want it but also being able to ignore it if it is not relevant.

Occasionally when I know a family well and they have suffered a loss I will ask if they would like to look in my 'Bereavement Box'. I explain that it is a box that can help us to talk about death and memories – sad ones and happy ones. I show it to them and then leave it available, but I never open it. I let them do that in their own time, if at all.

This is an activity to allow a conversation about death, bereavement and loss and make it okay to talk about these things; to give permission to play out the funeral, to ask questions and to express feelings. But it is not an activity to force families or children to discuss bereavement. If you do that, no matter how good your intention is, our practice is not safe.

Many of the items are used for free play or are just a visual aid for discussion/questions.

Other items can be connected to activities explained here:

- The owl puppet – 'Owls are wise and they know lots of things. If they can't answer a question they know how to find the answer. Do you have anything you want to ask the owl?'

- The candle – 'Let's light the candle to remember Granny (or whoever is being remembered). Look how pretty it is. Did Granny ever have any birthday candles? Did she have a candle in her house? Can you feel the warmth from the candle? That's like love. Love is warm. Is it nice? Now close your eyes. Can you remember what the candle looks like? Yes, you can! So now let's blow out the candle. Can you remember the warm feeling? Yes? Can you remember what the flame looked like? Yes? Well, that is just the same as when Granny died. She is not here to tell you that she loves you but she still does. Just like you still remember how warm the candle was and how the flame flickered. Even though Granny is not here now you can still talk about her and remember her.'

Helping with memories:

- The rainbow – 'Can you find a memory for all the colours in the rainbow?' For example, for 'red' it might be 'I remember Granny knitted me a red jumper', and so on. You might need to help a little to get started until the family gets the idea. Try and keep your example real. You may be able to say, 'I remember it was sunny the day your Granny died and there were blue skies.'

- The stones – a rough stone for a difficult memory; smooth for an everyday memory; precious for a very special occasion.

- The star box – I use this for the children to write or draw a memory and place it in the box and keep the box. We sometimes sing *Twinkle, Twinkle Little Star* as we fold the memory up and place it in the box with some ceremony.

Practice example

I was introduced to a father and five children after their mother had committed suicide. The children had found her. Everybody was traumatised but no one talked about Mum. I explained to Dad that it was important to give the children the opportunity to do this. He was willing but didn't know how to do it. I showed him the Bereavement Box when we were alone, which triggered emotions in him and we talked through his feelings and what he had told the children so far.

Later that day I returned to the home with my bag and let the children explore it. Cathy (7) and Leo (8), who had found Mum, immediately began to play with the items in the Bereavement Box and play out what they had seen. They showed Dad, who had not been at home when it happened. This was all that was needed to give them permission to talk. I helped only by supporting the play, suggesting a correct word occasionally and putting a hand on Dad's shoulder when he was struggling. We didn't use any of the activities that day as there was no need.

During the following few days Dad used the box to show the children what would happen at the funeral, including bringing Mum's ashes back in a jar. They would decide as a family when to 'let Mummy go' (scatter the ashes).

In the following weeks the children requested the box (they didn't want to keep it but did want me to bring it with me each visit). I saw this as a healthy way of controlling when they did talk about Mum as a family. Each time I visited we used some of the memory activities together.

Later in the summer holidays they made their own individual memory boxes with Dad and me helping. Dad also created a memory garden in their back yard.

The children subsequently attended a children's bereavement counselling project where they were delighted to show their counsellor some of the activities they had done.

VI. Mrs Doubtfire

This idea came from a parent. Sally didn't like the idea of having a social worker. She worked in a caring profession and the involvement of social services in her life challenged her identity. She was clear that she did not want the children (all under 9 years old) to know my job title. But she did recognise that she needed support and said she thought she could work with me. We had already had two sessions alone, but it was time for me to do some work with the children. I showed Sally the activities I would use and the purpose (initially for assessment) and she had no concerns about this but remained anxious they would find out my job title. She was afraid they would tell friends at school and also she said she didn't want to have to explain to them as adults why they had needed a social worker. After discussion she conceded that the second concern could not be hidden. The children would remember the domestic abuse and might well need to talk about it.

Nonetheless we still had a problem that was very significant to the point where Sally said she would disengage if the children had to know. I discovered that she had another fear which was that her parents would find out from the children. They were very important to her and an essential practical support. They didn't know the children had been placed on the Child Protection Register and would have been very disapproving, placing the blame on Sally.

I felt that the most important thing was that we worked together and the children got the support they needed. I decided that the children didn't really need to know my job title. I would explain to them that I was a safe adult who worked with children to help them sort out any muddles or worries. Sally accepted this but said she still needed to find a way of explaining my involvement to the children in a way she was comfortable with. I left her to think about it and the next day she got back to me, 'I can tell the kids you are like Mrs Doubtfire'.

I laughed but agreed and began to think how I could use this analogy. Mrs Doubtfire is a fictional children's nanny, who has lots of facial warts. As the problems besetting her charges are resolved, the warts disappear.

Sally had been open with her children about the problems she wanted me to help them with and I was keen to get their views on these. I therefore drew a picture of Mrs Doubtfire and in the first session asked Sally and the children to draw on warts and name the problems they represented. Sally drew a big angry-looking wart and stated, 'We need to stop Dad hurting me and keep you all safe.' The youngest, aged 4, drew a wart and said, 'Want Mummy to be happy.' The 7-year-old said, 'I love my dad and I want to see him more. I miss him.' We continued in this way until we agreed we had covered all the problems.

I then drew some medicine bottles and together we worked out the best medicine for each wart. Some of the medicine was 'for grownups to make and tell you about later' but I asked the children to help me draw some of their own solutions on the medicine bottles. We were able to agree that Dad could not come home or see the children as much as before, but the 'missing you' wart could be dealt with by sending a letter to him and having a weekly telephone call supervised by grandparents. We also decided that some of the medicine might be to have a photo of Dad beside their bed.

We worked on a couple of warts at a time and kept checking if the medicine was working or if we needed a different cure. Once the wart was cured, the children were invited to rub it out but I soon realised that this was too simplistic. Some problems had deeper roots which might take a long time to cure, if ever. But problems do sometimes quieten down for a while. I explained this as best I could to the children, saying that real problems didn't just disappear so easily. I suggested we attach a little piece of plain paper over the wart and then if the problem came back we could take it off and try something else. There were lots of nods and agreement.

So now we had a picture depicting a care plan but also a way of children showing us their needs and a parent who was happy to engage with me and relax in my company. This enabled her to feel safe enough to talk about her worries and things she needed help with and use the advice to improve her children's lives.

Practice example

This is not an activity as such, but rather an example to show how we can make use of analogy to help parents and children address difficult situations and/or change habits.

This was a single parent family with two teenage boys (13 years and 15 years). Dad and boys were very keen footballers who played several times a week. Dad was in recovery from an alcohol addiction and had come through a period in residential rehab. The boys had been in care for a year and a half and had now been home for six months. The honeymoon period was now over and the boys were beginning to test Dad's limits and boundaries. Dad, for his part, was doing well and providing adequate care. Although struggling with the boys' behaviour, he understood the need for consistent limits and boundaries and was trying to apply them. However, this was proving tough for him and he was at risk of running out of emotional energy to carry on.

Allan, the elder son, was finding it difficult to respect his father in the parental role. The last time he was living at home, during Dad's addiction period, he had taken on the parental role and had actually been the most able member of the family. Both boys tended to view Dad as a peer and although I needed Dad to take on the parental role, neither he nor the boys were ready to allow this to happen. As unpalatable as this was to me, it led me to think more creatively about how to help them get along better together, to function with less criticism of each other and more co-operation and kindness.

It came to me after I had just made a home visit where we had had some good, positive conversation where all family members had shown respect for each other and worked together. The subject of the conversation? Football. It was the one thing that united them. The following week I returned having worked on my knowledge of football, which *was* non-existent and still very basic.

I introduced the idea that they were not 'The Douglas Family' but in fact 'Team Douglas'. I spoke a little about football and asked them to assign roles to the team. Together they worked out:

Dad – Team manager/goalkeeper

Allan – Forward player

Kevin – Defender

Audrey – Coach/referee

Dad introduced the idea of red and yellow cards and we worked out which behaviour would bring out either one of the two cards.

This analogy really worked for the family. They were now able to talk through the subjects of responsibility, conflict and achievement in a calm and productive manner. I thought that this strategy would wear off after a while but I've been very wrong. Eighteen months down the line and they are still living as a family unit and continue to refer to themselves as 'Team Douglas'.

VII. My Twist on 'What's the Time, Mr Wolf?'
Purpose

- To support and encourage communication and dialogue about identity and qualities of the family group.

- This exercise provides you with a good assessment of family dynamics and general information about the family.

What you need

- A large space such as a garden, park or community centre.
- The ability to contain children in a large space and keep them working with you, so you need child management skills.

This is a group activity for three or more people.

What to do
The original version

1. One person in the group is picked to be Mr Wolf. This person stands at one end of the hall/garden etc. All the others stand in line some distance away, but near enough to hear Mr Wolf.

2. The group shouts, 'What's the time, Mr Wolf?'

3. Mr Wolf then replies (randomly picking a time), 'It's 3 o'clock.'

4. The group then takes three steps forward.

5. This is repeated, with the group moving forward the number of steps the 'wolf' gives.

6. As the group gets closer, the wolf picks the time to reply, 'It's DINNER time' and runs forward to try to catch someone while they run back as quickly as possible to the start line. The person who is captured is the new Mr Wolf and the game begins again.

It is a good idea to play this version before and after my version.

My family version

1. Set it up the same way with one Mr Wolf and a line of people. Draw a circle around Mr Wolf (or mark a circle with stones or bean bags). This is his den. (Tip: take a rope with you in case nothing else is found to use.)

2. Mr Wolf then has the task of shouting a statement and the family members take a step forward if they agree that the statement, in their view, is true and remain where they are if they disagree.

3. Mr Wolf has to try to win the game by getting all the family members into his den. You need to set a time limit for the game in case people don't move and you can award Mr Wolf a sticker/ praise/sweet for effort.

4. Once everyone is in the den there is a family celebration. This can be hugs; high fives; clapping or the worker could give everyone a sweet. I tend to do a combination of the above. Mr Wolf will be motivated to make accurate statements so that he wins.

The statements Mr Wolf makes should be positive, factual statements about the family. It can be a playful experience for a child to be able to control the family's movements when often they feel powerless. I think this may be one of the reasons the children enjoy this game.

Some examples of statements:

- We live in the high-rise flats.

- Mum loves chicken.

- I've been to three primary schools because we move so much.

- Emma likes to play with her dolls.

- Dad likes his beer.

- Mum visits Granny on Tuesdays.

- We are good at playing PlayStation

- We watch [a TV show] together.

- The electric ran out last week but Mum fixed it as she asked Nana for a loan.

If a family member stands still, Mr Wolf can ask why they are standing still by making a wolf howl. There can then be a time-limited period of discussion to and fro to try to resolve the differences in view. It may end up with some members moving forward but it always promotes some heated discussions and sometimes really positive resolutions. It is up to the worker to stay in control and ensure this remains emotionally safe for all members. You will also be making a note of all the statements which can be addressed more fully in a different setting at a later date. You can also stop the discussion if it becomes too heated. If you have a situation where not all family members reach the den then you don't have a celebration but Mr Wolf should be praised for the effort, and the family members not in the den thanked for their participation. It is very important to bring the group back together again and so we have a group 'howl' and usually a soft drink.

You can repeat the game with another Mr Wolf, or go back to play the original version. However, be mindful that there may still be unresolved tensions and judge whether another game of the family version is wise at that time. You might alter it a bit to add further safety, for instance ask Mr Wolf to confine statements to where we live. You should also try to leave space in your diary to make a follow-up home visit fairly quickly as it may have opened up some big issues. More often than not, though, it is not contentious and good fun.

Practice example

Using this game with a family, the 15½-year-old's statement was, 'We don't like it when Mum and you, Gran, argue.' The response was quite dramatic with all the children running into the den. Mum burst into tears and Gran stormed out of the community centre. Just at that moment I needed three of me.

Mum, the children and I sat around the table with a soft drink and biscuits and talked about the problem. The children and Mum described how Mum would run out of money and ask Gran for a loan. Gran would become angry, but of course there was more to it. Fortunately, Gran, having had a break, returned to the centre and while the children played with a ball in the centre I was able to talk to Mum and Gran, revealing a concern that Mum was drinking again, therefore running out of money and leaving the oldest child in charge of making tea, etc.

After our discussion it was still important to end the game properly so we had a group howl and paw shaking and stickers were given to the children. The family left in a good frame of mind, going to Gran's for a sleep-over as part of the safety plan for that evening, with a follow-up visit the next day and further work in the proceeding weeks.

VIII. Maslow's Boxes

This activity is also in our first book of activities for children. There it was used to help a mother understand the impact of neglect on her child. Here we show a practice example of how it was used to help a young couple understand why their first child was moved from their care and placed with adoptive parents and also help to begin an assessment of their ability to care for a second child on the way. For those not familiar with this activity, the instructions are repeated here.

What you need

- Seven lidded boxes, each a little smaller than the other so that when stacked they form a pyramid. If you are lucky you may find a set which comes packed together inside the biggest box. Otherwise a variety of small boxes with lids will do, as long as they stack on top of each other in decreasing size. Label each box on its side as follows, starting with the smallest at the top of the pyramid:
  ○ Being all you can be (self-actualisation).
  ○ Beauty, nature, balance, order and form (aesthetic need).
  ○ Knowledge, understanding, exploration, curiosity (cognitive needs).
  ○ Respect for self and others, feeling competent, self-esteem (esteem needs).
  ○ Receiving and giving love, affection, trust and acceptance (love and belonging).
  ○ Protection from danger, feeling safe (safety needs).
  ○ Basic needs such as food, drink, shelter etc. (physical needs). This is the largest box at the bottom of the pyramid.
- A lot of slips of paper, about two inches by one inch.
- Fine felt tip pens for writing with.

- A basic knowledge of Maslow's hierarchy of needs.[3]

- A confidential and quiet space, preferably with a table or flat surface.

- Enthusiasm – use of self.

What to do

1. Explain that you want to tell the person you are working with all about human needs. It's pretty cool and maybe even exciting once you get the hang of it. Ask them to help you place the boxes out on the table. You might encourage them at this stage to read the labels on the boxes. With a family where there are small children, see if they can find the smallest box, the largest box, the red box etc. It is important to have as much fun as possible and engage everyone, so lots of smiles and words of encouragement.

2. Say you want this to be fun but that also there is a serious side to it and there will be a lot of thinking needed. Tell them we are going to learn about psychology. If I am working with a child or young person I may say something like, 'I am going to tell you about a very wise man who lived a long time ago. He was curious and clever and fascinated by people. His name was Maslow, and he worked out what people need to grow and develop. Because he was kind he wrote it all down so we could learn to look after ourselves and each other.'

3. Ask the youngest child you are working with to put the boxes in order of size, starting with the largest box and laying them in a line on the table. Note that it has the label 'Physical needs'. Ask them to think of all the physical needs we require to keep alive and healthy and write them on the slips of paper and place them in the box. See if they can fill the box. You will need to support discussion around needs with ideas if appropriate. Try to personalise the activity to the client's situation, 'What are your baby's physical needs? What are yours, and are they different? Who made sure your physical needs were met when you were

---

3   See Gross, R. (2010) *Psychology: The Science of Mind and Behaviour*. London: Hodder Education.

a baby? Do you think your physical needs were met as a baby?
Can a baby meet their own needs or are they dependent on an
adult?' and so on.

4. Repeat the above with all the boxes, and as you go along place
   the filled boxes in a tower, starting always with the largest and
   working down in size. Engage the youngest children in discussion
   while the adults and older children write on the slips. Ask them
   what they need when their tummy rumbles or what does a baby
   need when it cries (a child of 3 or above would manage this
   question). They may like to draw a picture on a slip and 'post' it
   into the box.

   For assessment purposes you will have noted, as the boxes
   were being filled, where your clients had the most or the least
   difficulty.

5. Once your tower is complete (this may take up to an hour as
   people often find it challenging) make sure it is balanced well
   and standing firm.

6. This is where you explain in simple terms Maslow's theory that if
   one need was not met at the right time, then the next need could
   not be met properly and so development suffers as a child grows
   up. This might explain why some children have problems in life.
   Keep it relevant to your client's (or clients') issues. For example, in
   cases of physical neglect you point to the physical needs box and
   explain, 'Your child's physical needs are not being met just now.
   I know this because when I came yesterday the house was very
   cold and John had only a nappy on. He was cold to touch and he
   was crying because he was also hungry. This is what I mean by
   not meeting his physical needs.'

   Be blunt and straightforward and stick to facts. This is not
   being insensitive. It is being fair. Clients need to know clearly
   what the problems are. Sometimes professionals try to soften the
   blow by using lots of language or not being direct enough. It is
   human nature not to want to hear negative messages and clients
   either genuinely don't understand what is being said or mentally
   block more subtle messages and then get criticised when no
   changes are made.

7. Allow the client to think for a moment and then to challenge you on this observation if they wish. Repeat your message, giving another example if appropriate. Be clear and be firm but compassionate and respectful. Once any discussion that arises (if it does) has ended it is time to demonstrate the effects of this.

8. Pull the bottom box (physical needs) away from the pyramid. You can ask the client to do this or it could be a job for the youngest child. Observing the pyramid fall state, 'That's what is happening to your child's development.' Pause. 'It's falling down. His development is collapsing because his physical needs are not being met.'

    Often there will be a significant emotional reaction to this. It is a hard message to give and, being visual, it often touches people in a way words don't. Distress can be a catalyst for change, so if the client is upset allow this to happen. Don't try to comfort too soon. You need to use your own clinical judgement as to how long to allow this stage to last. This may require self-discipline, as some workers find it difficult to contain feelings of sadness or distress and come in too early to meet their own needs, not the client's. When you are ready, with lightness in your voice say something like, 'Come on. It is not all bad news. Look at this. You can always build the pyramid back up. You can really help your child and we can sort this problem out together.' If there is a child involved, ask them to build the pyramid up again or do it yourself. 'I know you can turn this around. I know you can meet his physical needs and the reason I know this is...' Give some positive feedback here based on fact – an observation or a report from another professional, remembering to note even the smallest positive action. 'When I asked you to get your child dressed and give him breakfast you did that and did it well. I also like the way I've seen you smile and cuddle him. But you need to meet his physical needs and I am here to help you work out how to do what I know you can do. So are you up for working with me on this one?'

9. Depending on the gravity of the situation you may want to point out here what the consequences would be if the parents continued

to fail to meet the child's needs, as you cannot continue to allow these needs to remain unmet.

10. Presuming you do get agreement from the parent to 'build the pyramid back up' and work towards meeting the child's needs, move to the first stage of task-centred practice.[4]

Practice example

A young, heavily pregnant woman answered the door when I knocked. She was immediately defensive, bordering on aggressive. Her partner, a young man in his late teens, stood behind her. She yelled, 'Just tell me, are you going to take my bairn off me?' I replied, 'What I can tell you is that I am always honest but as I don't know you yet I can't tell you if I am going to take your bairn off you.'[5] This was met with a brief silence whilst the young woman weighed me up as I stood on the doorstep. 'But you're going to tell me straight right now if you are going to take it off me.' 'I will be straight with you and the straightforward and honest answer is that I don't know yet. I need to get to know you both first. Now it is really cold out here [it was snowing] so are you going to let me in so we can get to know each other or am I going back to my car and marking this as a failed appointment? That wouldn't be a good start. Come on now, you make the choice.' I happened to know that both parents had been in residential care and thought I could see a flicker of recognition when I used the choices tactic.

Sure enough, after I was allowed to enter and sat down, the young man, Danny, asked, 'You worked in 'ressy' [residential care]?' I told him I had but that it was a long time ago. We had a brief chat about the residential establishments Danny had

---

4   See Lishman, J. (1991) *Handbook of Theory for Practice Teachers in Social Work.* London: Jessica Kingsley Publishers. The first stage of task-centred practice is to identify the tasks to be done.

5   Note the use of the same language as used by the young woman. This is intentional as a means of building a sense of connection with her; it is hoped that this is sending the message that we have some common ground even though still strangers.

lived in, those I had worked in and soon we had a common bond. I knew that Tammy and Danny would be expecting lots of questions but I felt this was not the best way to start. Experience has taught me that many clients have rehearsed answers, especially when they have had a history of social work involvement. I wanted them to relax as this would help me to reach a more accurate assessment.

The fact that their first child had been adopted felt a bit like the elephant in the room. We needed to acknowledge this – after all it was why I was there – but I also knew it would be painful to talk about.

'How's your pregnancy going, Tammy?'

'Good. I've kept all my appointments, I am eating well and my scans have all been normal.'

'Is it like your first pregnancy?'

'No, different. I love this baby. I mean really love it. I want it more than you can imagine. We got all the baby stuff in and Danny's working two jobs. I dinnae want to lose this one. I'll do anything you say just to keep this baby.'

'I hear you telling me that you really love your baby and you've been getting ready for the arrival and that you want to work with me and you want to keep the baby.'

'Yes.'

'I wonder…I would really like to hear your story of the first pregnancy and how you lost your first baby.'

Danny and Tammy described their first experience in detail. I let them talk, only interrupting occasionally to clarify a point. It was obviously difficult for them to talk about it but what became clear to me was that they hadn't processed information and so had no real idea of why their first baby had been adopted (without their consent). I was not unduly surprised as sometimes people go into survival mode when faced with awful experiences and it is hard for them to hear what professionals are telling them. Tammy and Danny had the words but they didn't have the meaning.

I was tempted to leave Maslow's boxes to the next meeting, but I also wanted to capitalise on the rapport we had been building so I decided to go ahead. I explained to Tammy and Danny that I wanted to help them understand what had happened, why social workers had decided to remove their baby and also give them the opportunity to show me how much they knew about caring for a baby. They showed an interest as I laid out the boxes, one on top of each other, each labelled with one step in Maslow's hierarchy of need. Danny and Tammy filled up most of the boxes with ease, showing their ability to understand what a child needs in terms of physical care, which was also confirmed by my observation of their home which was excellent in terms of hygiene and appearance.

Their ability to fill the emotional needs box was adequate but they were clearly uncomfortable and had to work a bit harder. They recognised this themselves and it gave me the opportunity to talk about their first child (records had noted, 'problems with bonding', 'not able to instinctively recognise what baby needs emotionally'). I gently put it to them that the social worker had been worried about how their love was growing for their first baby. What did they think?

Tammy said that she had thought that she had loved her baby but now wondered if this was not the case. She then quickly corrected herself and said no, she did love him, but that it feels different this time. 'I don't think I was ready last time.'

Danny said he loved both babies and was upset by Tammy's comments. I chose to depersonalise this a little by saying that Tammy had been a child herself during her first pregnancy and pointed out the dilemmas of pregnancy and how this may well have impacted on Tammy's experience of becoming a mum, especially when we considered that a lot of Tammy's own needs had not been met.

I used Maslow's tower to show both Tammy and Danny where I thought their needs had not been met. Both had experienced physical neglect in early years and been removed from their birth families and placed with foster families and subsequently residential care for Danny. We looked at how this would mean that the tower had fallen down and also had been rebuilt, but that it was still probably a wobbly tower. Both related to this and I reinforced that having bonding problems or difficulties with love growing was not anyone's fault but rather a symptom.

I could see Tammy visibly relax and Danny put his arm around her and his hand on her bump. Danny stated with conviction, 'But you know we love this baby. Can you help us with the love growing thing?'

I replied that I could see that the love had already begun to grow and it was probable that in three years they had moved on in their development and were ready to be parents now, but the love growing was only part of being a parent. I referred back to the boxes and how they had been filled. I gave them both praise for currently meeting the baby's physical needs. Tammy had attended all antenatal appointments, often supported by a friend or Danny; Danny was working two jobs saving up for the baby and they had showed me the baby's room which was brightly painted and had all the basic furniture for the baby including toys, nappies etc. However, it was important for me to be honest with them and say that there was still more assessment work to do and much of that could only take place after the baby was born.

Instead of being deflated, as I had feared, they both accepted this and said that at least I was being honest with them and that I was 'okay'.

After the baby's birth I took Maslow's boxes into the maternity ward. The midwives were very positive about the couple and had no concerns about the care of the baby. Before the discharge meeting I met the couple alone and asked them to show me with the boxes how they thought their baby's tower was standing. Danny took charge and built a very straight tower.

'It's strong,' he said.

I nodded. 'Yes, it is strong just now.'

'So, can we take her home?'

It was agreed they could but I said to them that I was still a bit worried that if a wind came along in the form of worries or practical problems, the tower might get wobbly, so I hoped they would agree to me visiting them and working together to keep the tower strong.

An agreement for close monitoring and co-operation was made. If there had been any problems at this stage the baby might not have been able to return home with them. Their child is now two years old and the health visitor says she is thriving. The couple are also now able to look at the painful feelings around the first adoption and are writing letters for their adopted child to see when older. Although there is no compulsory order in place any more they still come to see me occasionally and tell me how the tower is doing. Tammy was able to say that being able to see what the social worker was talking about really helped her to understand why people were worried and what she needed to do.

IX. Lemons and Lemonade
Purpose

- To help families identify their own resilient responses to hardships/difficult circumstances.

What you need

- Pens.

- Two sheets of flipchart paper, one with a lemon drawn on it and one with a bottle or glass of lemonade drawn on it.

What you do

I first saw this in a classroom in one of the high schools in Edinburgh. Under the picture of the lemon write, 'When life gives you lemons...' and under the picture of the lemonade write, 'Make lemonade!' Do this when the family is present. This activity is really aimed at the older children and adults, but don't exclude younger children. Help them to participate in the conversation and give them the job of colouring in or drawing more lemons to stick on.

Help the family to remember times when things were hard but they managed to find something positive in the situation. It is often easier to start with practical problems and then progress to discussing relationships issues or some of the tougher stuff. The important thing is to help the family to recognise their strengths and ability to cope. This is easier if you know them well because you will have examples to offer. A tip is to do it yourself before you try it with a family.

Figure 11.2: Lemons and lemonade

X. Rabbit Burrows
Purpose

- Creates opportunity to talk about family dynamics and the roles people have in families.

What you need
(There are templates for this activity in Appendix III.)

- A drawing of a rabbit burrow.

- Some card, pens and scissors.

- Adhesive to stick to the wall without marking it.

- Confidential space.

- Table. I prefer to work at a table but you can do this on the floor. Children often focus better when working at a table, I notice. They tend to be tempted to scoot around the floor instead of concentrating on the task.

What to do

1. Explain to the family that we are going to make a rabbit for each family member, including people who don't live in the home but are important people who visit frequently (e.g. grandparents, parents who live elsewhere or family friends).

2. Take time over this and give each rabbit some personal features. For example, Mum rabbit may have an earring because Mum wears earrings etc. I also find it helpful to write the person's name on their rabbit. I usually do this in small writing along the edge. It is really for the adult's benefit so that they can distinguish between similar rabbits belonging to the children. The other way of doing this is to use different coloured card and each person chooses one colour. Do ask the family to come up with their own ideas for decorating the rabbits. One family I worked with chose to put patterns on their rabbits. The boy loved football so his rabbit was covered with footballs. His older sister drew hair-straighteners all over hers!

3. Once you have designed the rabbits ask the family to think about what their rabbits might need in their burrows. You are looking for things that might meet basic physical needs like food, bedding etc. but allow imagination to run as long as you have some things which are basic to family life. One little girl aged 9 told me the rabbits would definitely need a periscope. She drew one and we cut it out. When I asked why they would need this I was told, 'To watch out for hunters.' At a later date the same child showed me the toy binoculars she used as a small child to watch out the window for her Dad coming.

4. Once you have all the rabbits and the practical items, ask the family to place them on the burrow in the positions where they think they should be. Invite each family member to make up a story about the Smith Rabbit family (use their own family name). It is surprising how often you will hear real-life stories emerging. You can also ask the family questions like, 'Now all the rabbits are hungry. Which rabbit will go and get the food, and make sure everybody has tea?' Encourage the family to play out what

happens when you have done that. Ask, 'Was that what happens in your house or was that just pretend?' Or, 'The little rabbit's fur is dirty. Who is going to help with that?'

5. You could introduce a fox and explain that the fox is a danger to the rabbit family. I know this sounds obvious but don't assume your family knows this if the parents have had very little schooling or poor concentration in school. Their general knowledge may be very limited. These days you would hope not, but just a few weeks ago I was present when a little girl of 5 asked her mum, 'What's snow made of?' and Mum replied, 'I don't know' and this is in Scotland where we see snow every winter. I gave the answer; it was a privilege to see how much interest Mum and daughter showed and this resulted in a lovely conversation about weather.

6. Make the fox prowl around. Usually there will be a spontaneous response. One mum I was working with quickly used her rabbit to gather up all the little rabbits in her hand and announced, 'You are not getting my babies,' at which point the children, aged 4 and 6 years, climbed onto her knee and there was a big family cuddle. We then talked about real family life and explored situations where Mum had protected her children and the children were able to tell me about 'bathroom cuddle time'. This was when Mum would take them into the bathroom and lock the door and call the police when her partner became abusive. They had 'bathroom cuddle time' until help arrived.

You can also help the family to consider alliances in the family group. Who spends time together? Does anyone feel left out? You can do this by asking each family member to place all the rabbits into the burrow. Who is going to play in the tunnels? Who will spend time in the nests? While one person does this ask the others to watch silently and they will have their turn next.

Practice example

One little boy I worked with placed his rabbit on the grass and his mum and sister rabbits in a nest in the burrow. I reflected back what I saw.

Me: 'The Jordan rabbit is alone outside the burrow and Mum rabbit and Joanne rabbit are snuggled up inside.'

Jordan: 'Yes.'

Me: 'Can you tell us or show us more?'

No response from Jordan. It was possibly too abstract a request. So I tried another open-ended request: 'Show us what happened next.'

Jordan shows his rabbit playing on the grass for a while and then attempting to join Mum and Joanne rabbits. Mum rabbit tells Jordan rabbit to go away and do your homework. Joanne rabbit pushes Jordan rabbit away.

Me: 'How did Jordan rabbit feel?'

Jordan: 'Sad. No one wants me.'

Mum at this point interjects and says that is not true and that Jordan never does his homework and never listens to her.

Jordan picks up his rabbit and throws it, 'I can't do it. It's too hard. You won't help me. I hate you!'

Mum cries and explains the issue is with maths homework. She can't help because she can't do it and as we talk I discover this has been going on for a few weeks. Jordan has been refusing to come in from play because it is homework time and he needs help which mum won't give because she can't. They then fall out. Jordan eventually feels excluded from the family group. Like a lot of problems, once this was aired it was pretty easy to fix. I asked Mum to tell Jordan honestly why she didn't help and give him a hug and we agreed to approach school. Jordan began after-school club, and I planned some one-to-one time for Jordan and Mum while Joanne went to Girl Scouts.

In the wider scheme of things this seems a minor problem for children who were on the Child Protection Register. But sorting this out alleviated daily stress and strengthened relationships in the family, which is protective. It is important not to overlook what can be perceived as 'little problems' that relate to ordinary family life because sorting out the detail can have a very positive impact on daily life.

It is also important to assess how the family dealt with this. I noted that neither Jordan nor his Mum had asked for help until we did this activity and it was Jordan who reached out. Mum had actively tried to conceal the issue. At a later date I gently shared this reflection with Mum, explaining that as human beings we have behaviour patterns. Was there anything else she was worried about and not sharing? Mum presented as defensive that day and adamant that there were no other issues. However, at the following appointment, having had time to think about it, she told me about several other problems that she had concealed.

Final thoughts

- Do use your imagination as not everybody will relate to rabbits and burrows. One of my families liked frogs so I did the same exercise with frogs in a pond with lily pads. Meerkats in burrows is a popular one as they are on TV a lot.

- You just need a family group and an environment which offers separate spaces, and the internet will supply images/cartoons to help you create your templates.

XI. Interviewing the Family Pet or Soft Toys

Establishing a rapport with families when we are given very little time can be difficult. Often we are strangers to the home so we shouldn't expect to be welcomed in and taken into their confidence immediately (it is in fact a cause for concern if they do). However, especially when children are involved, we sometimes encounter situations where change needs to occur as quickly as possible. As anyone who has worked with children will know, using other objects to talk with them about difficult things indirectly can work very well. Children often find it easier to open up to a puppet or toy (operated by you) spontaneously.

I have also found that it can work with adults too. The best way to explain how I use this technique is to give practice examples.

Practice examples
Interviewing the family pets

John had four children under 12 years old and significant mental ill health. He was a single parent and had worked with a social worker for about a year and a half until she left. As John had been managing to meet his children's needs and they had support from a counsellor based in school and he had a Community Psychiatric Nurse to continue to support him, the practice team did not reallocate the children to a new social worker.

However, a new referral came into the duty team from the school. The children were looking unkempt, often late for school and having more absences than had been the usual pattern. As duty social worker that day it was my job to do a home visit and begin an assessment. I read the case notes in preparation for the visit and noted that the youngest child attended one of our child and family centres. I called his key worker who gave me an account of the current circumstances and most helpfully some anecdotal information, particularly about the child's likes and dislikes. So at least I would go with a few clues as to what might catch their interest and help me, a stranger, to engage with them. Just before I ended the call, the key worker said, 'Oh, by the way Audrey, there are two dogs, one called Max and the other Sophie. Whatever you do don't ask them to be put in another room or ignore them. John will judge you on how you are with the dogs.'

Now I had a real challenge on my hands. Being less than confident with dogs I generally didn't engage with them and often asked for them to be put in another room while I sussed out if they were safe/friendly. I made a quick call back to the key worker to ask what the dogs were like and was told that they sounded fierce but were 'big softies' once you established who was boss. 'Just be firm with them, Audrey, and you will be fine.'

So I arrived at the house, rang the door bell and could hear the two dogs howling at the door and barking. This was my worst nightmare but I decided I had to be positive and trust what I had been told about the dogs and be firm. Just then John opened the door. He held Max, a Rottweiler, by the collar and Sophie, a mixed breed, with the other hand.

We made brief introductions and he invited me in.

'These are lovely dogs, John, what are their names?'

'Max and Sophie. You like dogs?'

'Yes, I do,' I assured him honestly (I do like dogs, just not their teeth) but didn't say I was actually frightened of them and trying hard to mask this.

John let the dogs go and they bounded towards me, tails wagging.

Although pretty scared I decided to try to be firm, and after a few attempts which didn't achieve anything I said, 'Sit' firmly and to my surprise and relief they did. After a few friendly overtures to the dogs, John called them to him and ordered them to lie down, which they did and we got on with the reason for the visit. John, who was alone in the house, was aware of why I was there. He summed it up for me.

'Know why you are here. Kids are off school more than they should be, they are not clean enough according to the busy-bodies and they don't like how I live but they are my kids and it is my house and I'll live how I like. The kids are fine so you can go away.'

I was sitting on top of rubbish – empty crisp packets and other detritus strewn over the sofa. I couldn't really see any of the floor and the house smelled stale (urine, dog and old food). The school had reported the children's personal hygiene as poor. Clearly we had a bit of a problem. I needed to effect a change here.

I didn't want to start with confrontation. It was not going to get us anywhere. John had a habit of throwing workers out of his home and I suspected this option was on the horizon. I had to think quickly.

Me:	'How are the dogs, John?'
John:	'The dogs?'
Me:	'Yes, I would love to know more about them. What do they like to do?'
John:	'They are good dogs. They like to be with me. They can do tricks.'
Me:	'Oh, what kind?'
John:	'Sophie can die for her country.'
Me:	'Oh, you mean roll over and act like she is dead?'
John:	'Aye.'
Me:	'Could you show me?'
John:	'Aye. Well...no.'
Me:	'Oh, why not?'
John:	'Well, it is a bit difficult. She needs space.'
Me:	'Ah, well...could we make space, what do you think, Sophie?'

The dog pricked up her ears at the sound of her name. 'Would you not like your daddy to tidy a wee space for you? You must be awfully uncomfortable lying in the rubbish...'

John was listening and watching the dogs. I noticed Sophie had a cut paw. 'Oh, Sophie, you have cut your paw. Poor wee thing. Did you cut it on a walk or in the house, I wonder? There are some sharp things here. It is not very safe for you or the children, huh?'

Sophie at this point wandered over to me and I bent down, feeling a bit braver as both dogs were relaxed. 'Oh, hello, darling. What's that you are saying? You would like Dad to clean up so you and the children have got space to play. I think you are a wise dog. It must be hard for you and the children to move round the house. But you know what, Sophie, it can be hard for people to get started. Now, Sophie, would you let me get your dad some help just to get this started?' I looked up at John.

John: 'I don't like folk in my house nosing around my things.'

I patted Sophie. 'Sophie, what do you think we should do? I think your dad is a person who likes his privacy. Mmmm, Sophie, do you think if we just got help with the kitchen and bathroom first, that might help?'

I looked at John who was patting Max and making no response. Oh dear, I thought, I am losing this. But I carried on, 'You see, Sophie, the children might get hurt, or fall over something just like you have cut your paw or they might get sick if they eat food that's not been prepared on a clean surface. We need to help your dad fix this. I wonder what would help.'

At this point Sophie got bored of me and walked back to John.

'Oh good girl, you are going to ask your dad what I can do to help.'

At this point John looked at me directly and said, 'You're a bit weird, are you no?'

I smiled back, 'Yes, I suppose so but we need to work together, John, you and I both know that, don't we?'

John nodded.

Me: 'Okay, time for straight talking. The kids need better than this and you and Sophie and Max do too. We need to sort out this home now, John. It can't wait and it is not like you to let it get this bad. So what do I need to do to help you get back on track? What's up? What's got you to this place? You tell me. You are the expert on yourself and your family.'

John shrugged, 'Give me a couple of days and I will sort it out.'

Me: 'Okay. Kitchen and bathroom first. No change by Friday and we will do it my way and get folk in to help you. Deal?'

John: 'Aye.'

Me: 'Right, Sophie and Max, you keep him organised. I want to see you do your tricks on Friday.'

I left, returning on Friday. In short, some work had been done but not enough. We agreed the children would go to stay with Granny until the home was cleaned and made safe. Initially John didn't agree to any assistance. The children were returned six weeks later by which time the work in the house had been done and I had begun to establish a relationship with the children.

I discovered that Max and Sophie were very important in their lives too. Connie (9) told me that Max listened to her and got her up for school in the morning by barking. I suspected he wanted his breakfast as this was Connie's job. This made me question what happened in the morning. Support workers were introduced to help establish a morning routine.

On home visits the children and John were often quite guarded around me. So I got into the habit of asking, 'Who is going to help Max and Sophie tell me about the last week (or tell me about why the police came to your house yesterday etc.). A child would go and sit by the dog, placing an arm round its neck, whisper in the dog's ear and then speak for the dog. This proved to be a safe way for the family to tell me what was going on.

Using soft toys

Ayesha was 10 years old and she had no reason to trust adults. She was keeping herself safe and was determined not to entertain me when I talked to her. She put her hands over her ears. When I invited her to look in my big work/toy bag she kicked it. If I attempted to work with her in school, she wouldn't approach me or alternatively just swept everything off the table with a look of challenge in her eyes.

Mum, Lizzie, was pretty resistant to social work too and I suspected that Ayesha had been told lots of negative untruths about social workers. After some weeks of patient persistence she was letting me visit, keeping most of her appointments, but whenever I began to talk about concerns she tried to direct the conversation by displays of anger and asking me to leave.

Ayesha had serious health problems and she needed to attend the hospital. This hadn't been happening and school attendance was poor. We wondered if she was becoming unwell.

On the next home visit I took my bear with me. It is a big bear and if you rub his nose, ears, toes or tummy he moves and makes noises. Most children and adults like him. Lizzie opened the door to find me holding the bear and smiling. She smiled back and asked, 'What's that?'

I didn't answer immediately as I wanted to get in first. Ayesha's bedroom door opened into the hall and I wanted to answer the question as I walked past in the hope she would hear and be curious. So at first I just laughed and as I walked past the bedroom said, 'This, Lizzie, is my bear.' As I said this I touched his ears and the bear laughed too. Lizzie was taken with him, 'I like that. Does he do other stuff too?'

Me, 'Yes he does – but he is very special to me so I only bring him to families I trust.'

'Oh, aye,' said Lizzie.

So Lizzie and I went into the living room and began to talk. There had been a fourth missed hospital appointment and I broached this subject. I still had the bear on my knee and I was stroking him gently (puppet work is most effective when you work in a way that suggests you have a relationship with the toy). Just then, Ayesha's head popped round the door. I deliberately ignored her as I wanted her to come to me. I tickled the bear's paw and it made a funny sound. I continued my conversation with Lizzie. Ayesha came into the living room and ran towards me and tried to grab the bear. I said firmly, 'No, you can't have him if you are going to grab him. He is very special to me and he is sick. Ayesha, I can't give him to you if you are going to be unkind or rough. You understand, Lizzie, don't you?' I was taking a bit of chance here that Lizzie would agree but it was worth the risk as I wanted to include both mother and daughter. But also significantly I was taking control and establishing boundaries and looking for co-operation both from the child and the adult. I had also begun to look empathically at the bear who was sick with a sore tummy just like Ayesha and needed care, just like she did, so I was modelling caring behaviour.

'Behave yourself, Ayesha,' replied Lizzie.

I now turned to Ayesha.

Me: 'You see this little bear has a sore tummy and we need to be gentle with him and not hurt him.'

Ayesha: 'I like soft toys. I've got lots on my bed.'

Lizzie: 'Aye, too many. You can hardly get into your bed.'

Me: 'Would you like to bring one through and introduce it to my bear?'

Now I am offering the child some control. I am attempting to build partnership.

So Ayesha introduced my bear to her 'raggy bunny' and eventually I was invited into her room to visit her soft toys. There were lots of them and I was introduced to each one of them. I was informed of who had given them to her and what their likes and dislikes were. I listened, shook paws, admired colour or fur and occasionally I was allowed to hold and cuddle one of the toys. I noticed that there were some under the bed covers which had not been brought out and I was curious as to why. I poked my bear's nose under the covers and brought him quickly back out again, raising him to my ear and pretending to listen intently. Then I said, 'Bear says there are more cuddly friends under the covers. He'd like to meet them.'

Ayesha looked at me. I wasn't sure what the look conveyed: anger, fear, puzzlement? I wasn't sure but there were strong emotions. I didn't want to push too hard so just sat Bear on my knee at a jaunty angle and waited with positive anticipation.

Ayesha pulled the covers back and there under the covers were three soft toys, a toy gun and a baby's dummy.

I initially focused on the soft toys although I was more curious about the toy gun, engaging Bear in shaking paws with each of them. Once that was done I moved him towards the dummy and toy gun (which incidentally looked very real). I had Bear look at these objects and then lifted him to my ear.

'Oh, you are asking me what these things are. That's a dummy and that is a toy gun.'

At this point Ayesha exclaimed, 'It's my dummy and my toy gun and it really works so don't touch it.'

I made Bear shake his head and whisper in my ear.

Me: 'Oh you are a wee bit scared and you want to tell Ayesha you are sorry if you upset her. You think the gun looks very real and hard to cuddle up to.'

Ayesha: 'Aye, well it keeps me safe when bad stuff happens, so there.'

Bear to my ear: 'You want Ayesha to know that you have known other children who have had bad stuff happen to them and that I might be able to help if she could tell us about the bad stuff.'

Ayesha at this point is watching me intently. I am focusing on Bear and deliberately making no eye contact and keeping my fingers crossed that nobody interrupts us at this moment.

Ayesha lifts up her own teddy bear which was under the covers and lifts it to her ear.

'I've got to tell them why they can't help 'cause only you can see the bad people and you and me we shot them with the gun and I suck my dummy and go to sleep again like when I was a wee bairn.'

My bear goes over to Ayesha's bear: 'Tell me what they look like.'

'Oh, I don't know,' says her bear, 'Ayesha sees them when she is dreaming. It's scary for her and then she wakes up and she holds me and the gun and we shoot them.'

My bear: 'Do they come every night?'

Ayesha's bear: 'No, just when her mum makes her watch the ghost programmes.'

Further discussion between the bears revealed that Ayesha's mum liked watching *Most Haunted*, a TV programme about investigators looking for ghosts in people's houses or communities and Lizzie insisted that Ayesha watch it with her 'so they could look after each other'. On the nights this show was on Ayesha had nightmares and was very afraid. She hadn't told her mum but finally did tell her that Bear was scared and Mum's response had been to ridicule Bear and then provide him with a toy gun to protect him.

Ayesha was very clear she couldn't tell her mum that she was frightened and she was also clear she didn't want me to address this issue with her mum. Lizzie was reluctant to engage with any social worker and I was at the start of an assessment process, but I had already got a sense that Lizzie was harsh with Ayesha and not always in tune with her needs. I had a dilemma. Clearly being exposed to an adult programme which was frightening her needed to stop and clearly I needed to address this. However, Ayesha had a good measure of her mum and was very clear she didn't want me to do that. Addressing this head on would risk Lizzie disengaging and where would that leave Ayesha who had only just felt able to engage with me and share something she was unhappy with? If I didn't address it (not that that was ever an option), I would be ineffective and collusive. So how could I address it without breaking Ayesha's trust and reducing the risk of Lizzie disengaging?

I looked at Ayesha who was by now looking very worried.

Me: 'Ayesha, do you and Mum ever play with your soft toys together, like we've been doing?'

Ayesha: 'Yeah, sometimes though not so much now. She says I am getting older and it is so embarrassing.'

Me: 'Hmmm. Why don't we make up a story about watching *Most Haunted* and getting scared and use the bears to play it out and show to Mum?'

Ayesha: 'Maybe…'

Me: 'It would be cool. I think your mum would like to see how clever you are.'

Ayesha: 'Maybe. Well, when would we do it?'

Me: 'Now. Let's get started. Which bear will be the mummy and which will be the baby?'

So together we made up a little re-enactment. It only took about 15 minutes and a social worker bear was included: 'Oh dear oh dear, baby bears are not allowed to watch adult programmes until they are at least 16 years old and as of today, no more *Most Haunted* for you, baby bear, even if you want to watch, mummy bear must say, No!'

So Ayesha and I played this out to Lizzie who got the message. She picked up mummy bear and said, 'And I say social workers should keep out of my business,' this said with humour and a smile.

I smiled back but also gave a look which I hoped conveyed I was serious and I was pleased when this was followed by the bear being placed down and Lizzie saying, 'Aye, I know she won't see it again. Now, you remember, Ayesha, you've got to go to your bed and no messing around.'

At this point I backed up Mum, reminding Ayesha, much to her annoyance, that 9pm on a school night was late enough.

On that occasion this method worked. Lizzie and Ayesha continued to engage with me and while the relationship building and change work was never easy and often challenging it did happen and teddies were a fairly regular feature of our home visits.

XII. Family Tree
Purpose

- A fun activity for adults and children. It helps create a sense of belonging.

What you need

- A large canvas, bought from a craft shop. The larger the family, the bigger the canvas required.

- Acrylic paint in as many colours as there are family members.

- Plates – one for each colour of paint. Strong, disposable cardboard plates can be used if a quick tidy-up is needed.

- A brush.

- Protective clothing and easy access to a sink.

What to do

1. Draw a tree trunk on the canvas.

2. Let the family members choose a colour each and start by putting one colour onto the plate. Invite the person who chose the colour to lay their hand onto the plate to get a good covering of paint and then place their hand carefully onto the top of the tree trunk.

3. Each family member follows, adding their own handprint in their chosen colour and before you know it you have a family tree.

This is a lovely activity to do with a family but perhaps especially when working with children in foster care. It helps to give them a visual and tactile experience of belonging to the foster family. As they grow up, hands get bigger and they can measure this against the picture, marking the time they have been in the family.

When the paint is dry I like to write the names against the handprints in permanent marker.

Further activity

A similar activity to this is to paint onto white porcelain. You can buy cheap mugs and plates from supermarkets and porcelain paint can be bought in craft or art shops. It is great fun to make a family plate, writing everybody's names around the rim. Young children can paint a simple picture instead of writing or put a handprint on a mug.

XIII. Footprints

(This activity was contributed by Becky Dunn, a children and families social worker in Edinburgh – see Chapter 8.)

Purpose

- To help children and their families to reflect on significant events and people, and the role these have had in their life.

- To support children and their families to have increased understanding for each other's experiences.

What you need

- For each individual taking part in the exercise you will need up to 10 'stop sign' cards and 10 'footprints' cards. These ideally will be approximately A5 to A4 size.

- Pens/pencils.

- Physical space to lay out the cards.

What to do

1. At the start of the activity, explain to those taking part that life stories can be understood as a series of different events. Also key to life stories are the role of individuals. You may want to give an example to illustrate this such as the birth of a new child in the family (event), or the role of a significant teacher in a child's life (individual). You also need to explain that events and individuals can be experienced as positive influences on the life story (footprints) or negative influences (stop signs). It is important to point out that one person's experience of an event or individual may be different to another. Again in using the example of the birth of a new child, the mother may view this as a positive (footprint), whereas the sibling of this new child may view this as a negative (stop sign).

2. Next, give each individual up to 10 footprint cards and 10 stop sign cards. Ask them to think about the significant events and

individuals in their lives that they felt either acted as a positive influence in their life or as a negative influence. Ask them to note these down on the cards, either as a footprint or as a stop sign.

3. Once they have done this, ask them to put these cards into a timeline in chronological order, laying them down on the ground in a line, with the earliest event closest to them, and the most recent farthest away. Ask each individual to then talk through what they have written down.

4. At this point, your role is to help the individuals involved to reflect on what they and their relatives have written. It is important to facilitate this so that throughout the activity, respect for each other's experiences and views is maintained. The focus of the reflection and the discussion that takes place will vary depending on the individuals involved but these are some suggestions:

   ◦ Look for patterns: is there a place on each timeline where there were multiple footprints or stop signs in a row? Explore why that might have been the case. How did they feel about that time in their life? How was that time experienced by the others taking part?

   ◦ Compare and contrast: where relatives have had shared life experiences, what has been similar and what has been different? Did one individual experience an event as a 'footprint' whereas another experienced it as a 'stop sign'? Did one individual experience this event or individual in the context of many other positive experiences or many other negative experiences? Support those taking part to understand better the experience of each other.

   ◦ Play 'God': ask the individuals to take out one 'stop sign' of their choice. Ask those taking part to imagine what difference that might have made to their life story and those around them.

   ◦ Ranking: explore what was the most important of the 'footprints' and 'stop signs' for each person and why. You might want to explore how the timing of a 'footprint' or 'stop sign' impacted upon the life story.

Practice example

John (12) and Alice (14) are siblings who are living at home with their father Peter. Three years ago John and Alice's mother Elizabeth died. In the months following Elizabeth's death, Peter struggled to cope and started using illicit substances. The Children and Families' Department became aware when Peter picked up the children from school (who were then aged 9 and 11) under the influence of substances. The children were accommodated into foster care. A rehabilitation plan was attempted and after nine months in foster care, the children were returned home to their father's care. The children are both trying to understand their life story, but Peter is finding it difficult to support this due to his own strong feelings about what happened.

In this activity, the children and Peter all note that Elizabeth's death was a 'stop sign' in their life. In the time leading up to Elizabeth's death, Peter has noted a number of 'stop signs' including the death of his mother and the loss of his job. I explored with the family how the events leading up to Elizabeth's death had made her death even more difficult for Peter to cope with. Peter states that he hasn't ever thought about this, and is able to see that this had contributed to his relapse into heroin use. Whilst Peter puts the children going into foster care as a 'stop sign' as well, the children have put this down as a 'footprint'. Through exploration, the children are able to articulate that they felt that this experience gave 'Dad a shock' and made him stop using heroin. John had put his teacher down as a 'footprint' because the teacher had been someone he could talk to, and John had a number of other 'footprints' during the time he went into foster care. Alice, however, had few footprints around this time. Peter later told me that he thought that this might explain why Alice had seemed to struggle more whilst in foster care than her brother.

The activity helped the family to better understand not only their own experiences and life story but also those of each other. I also had an increased understanding of the subjective experiences of the children and their father. This understanding helped inform both assessment of the children's needs and what future support might be beneficial.

XIV. Contact Targets

Purpose

- To try to obtain a child's view about contact arrangements with family.

What you need

- A large piece of paper.
- Pens.
- Small circles of card with a diameter of approximately 3cm (1 inch).
- Reusable adhesive.
- Boxes (optional).

What to do

1. On the paper draw a target. You will need eight rings to write in so make eight circles of decreasing size (see Figure 11.3). I usually have this prepared before I meet the child.

2. In the centre you will write:

   ○ people I see almost every day.

   Then working out from the centre:

   ○ people I want to see every day

   ○ people I want to see every week

   ○ people I want to see once in a while

   ○ people I want to see about once a year

   ○ people I want to Facebook/Skype

   ○ people I want to phone/email or write a letter to but don't want to see

   ○ people I think of but don't want to have any contact with.

3. When using the target you may find that some children, depending on age and development, find it difficult to understand the concept of time. If this is the case with the child you are working with you might want to relate the time frame to something else in their life. For example:

    ◦ 'Every week – like you see Auntie Jean.'

    ◦ 'About once a year – you have your birthday once a year.'

4. You will also have brought with you circles of card prepared earlier, with pens and reusable adhesive. Invite the child to think of everyone in their life, including people/family they live with and ones they don't live with; people they see and don't see. Include friends, teachers, social workers etc. Write each name on a circle of card.

5. Now invite the child to begin to place the people in the right circle. Read out what is written in each circle a few times and repeat as you go, even if you are working with a child who appears to read well, as you want the child to concentrate on placing the cards, not trying to read words.

6. I recommend that you start with people the child knows well and sees most days, including the people they live with and presumably the teachers and friends they attend school with. This gives them practice at placing the circles and understanding what to do. You can attach the circles with the reusable adhesive so they don't get knocked off the paper as you work. You could write directly onto the target but the problem with this is that it doesn't allow for changes or mistakes.

7. You should end up with a complete target which gives the child's views about contact – on that day! It is important to recognise that. There will be many influences at play which will influence the child's views. There will be normal childhood ups and downs with friends. But there is also likely to be significant family pressure in respect of contact when, for example, parents live apart. Children are sensitive to family mood and most children want to please their main care giver. They will also be aware of your role and may want to try to please you. It is very likely that

they will have mixed feelings about contact with certain people and we need to allow for this. Try to emphasise that you know that they may have mixed-up feelings as well as angry, happy, excited and sad feelings and all of those are okay.

8. Also explain that you know that they may change their minds because of that. When finished, take it away and bring it back another day to do it again.

9. When you take it away, photocopy it or note their answers down. Bring it back with the circles of card taken off the target to do again. Look for recurring themes. Some children won't want to do it again and if that is the case don't push it, just accept that. If you push you will become an unsafe adult to them and trust will be broken.

10. Another thing to be aware of is that all the options I have written on the target may not be available for every person the child knows. For example they may not be able to see Gran every week because she lives too far away. Don't try to correct that while they are working on the target. This is unhelpful because it implies that there is a right/wrong answer and places more pressure on a child as they grapple with what, for most children, will be a hard task. Wait until they are finished when you review it with them. You might say something like, 'Oh, I see you wish to see your Gran who lives in Orkney every week. Tell me about her.'

11. Once the child has talked about Gran, 'Sounds like you enjoy Gran's company and you want to see her more but we can't get you to Orkney every week, sorry. But I bet we could organise a phone call every week and you could visit your Gran once in a while. What do you think?'

12. In addition, in some situations it is important to explain to the child that you want to know what they think and what they want to happen but you can't promise that will happen. Explain clearly why that is. For example, 'Mum has to say what she wants to happen too and the judge who is very wise will decide.' Try when possible to give a time frame, for example, 'We will know

by the summer holidays.' If you don't know when the decision will be made, say so.

Another way to do the same exercise is to use boxes, writing the options on the outside of each box and asking the child to 'post' the names of the people into the box. The advantage of this is that the child only has to focus on one person at a time and does not have a visual reminder of their other choices. For example, times to visit Mum compared to times to visit Dad. This option can work well for children who are very concerned about what others may feel and also for children who have poor concentration and cope better with just focusing on one thing at a time, that is, a card in hand and looking at one box at a time, rather than being faced by an array of choices all on the one page, as would be the case with the target.

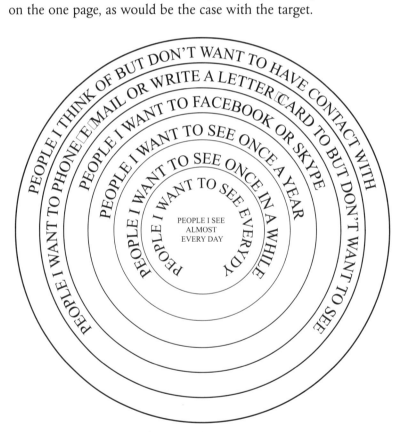

Figure 11.3: Contact target

XV. Loving Hearts
Purpose

- This highlights to parents and children the practical things people do that are demonstrations of love and care.

- By doing this you hope to open up discussion about relationships and increase positive behaviour.

What you need

- Heart shapes cut out of colourful card.

- Pens.

- Sticky tape.

- If there are children under 8 in the family group, bring glue sticks which are safe for children, glitter, bits of fabric, shiny things so they can simply decorate hearts if they are not able to join in fully.

- An uninterrupted space.

- Snacks and drinks.

What to do

1. Explain to everyone that you are going to talk about different ways people show that they love each other. (Incidentally this is a nice activity to do on Valentine's Day, especially if the family you are working with is very sensitive about any implication that they need support in areas of emotional care/literacy. It can be a sensitive subject but presented on the day which everyone celebrates love, it becomes less threatening and more acceptable. If it brings giggles or smart comments from the teenagers, just go with it.)

2. Give everybody some hearts. Always include the little ones. Children as young as 12 months can hold a crayon and scribble; at 2 years and above they can use a glue stick and stick things onto hearts. They can then be invited to give this to someone

in the group (sometimes this happens spontaneously) and this is their demonstration of love – to give away their art work.

3. For children who are not yet able to write or are not confident about writing, which could of course apply to adults too, they can draw onto a heart. Anyone can draw a stick figure – for the adults who protest they can't draw. Alternatively they can cut pictures out of magazines to represent what they are wishing to convey and stick those onto the hearts. The worker can help by adding a sentence dictated by the participant.

4. Begin by explaining that we all do practical things to show that we care about or love each other. Give some examples that relate to you but are not too personal. There is value in this. Our clients are often fascinated about us and we ask them to talk about things that are very personal. Sharing snippets of information helps to build relationships, mutual trust and respect. So I might say things like:

   ◦ I show my cat I love him by stroking him gently, talking to him, feeding him and making sure he has a comfy bed.

   ◦ I show my best friend I care about her by always remembering to send her a birthday card, listening to her worries and laughing with her.

   ◦ I show my partner I love him by making his packed lunch every day; by spending time with him, by telling him I love him etc.

     You notice that most of the personal examples could be said by many people. I've not given any names or detail and although personal to me I have divulged very little. A balance between creating relationship building and remaining professional has been maintained.

     You will notice also that in my examples I have included *tasks* – a comfy bed for the cat; a birthday card bought; making packed lunch and then *emotional care* – talking to him; listening to worries and laughing; spending time and telling him I love him. I am modelling here: giving examples of what the family might write, explaining and pointing out what the practical demonstration of love and care can be.

5. Next begin to try and create discussion with the family. Help as much as you can. People often lack confidence and are frightened to give a wrong answer. Try giving examples of what you have observed that relates to them. For example:

    ○ 'When I arrived today I saw Graham changing Gary's nappy. That's a demonstration of care and love. If you didn't care about Gary, you would leave him feeling uncomfortable.'

    ○ 'On the last visit I made, I saw Louise hug Laura when she fell. Why did you do that, Louise? What were you feeling?'

6. Once people start to engage in the conversation, get them to write/draw onto the hearts. Have lots of heart shapes available and good pens in working order.

7. Encourage people to make lots of hearts by writing as many things as they want to. A word of advice – people often write two to three examples on one heart, for example, 'I get John up for school, make his breakfast and take him to school. I always make sure he has got his lunch money.' There are four potential hearts in there. We want to really emphasise how important each action is and the feeling behind it. We need to capitalise on the examples we have, especially as some families will struggle, so help them to identify the different examples in one statement and make hearts for each one. Family members are also likely to copy each other's examples – that's just fine. So if Mum writes, 'I make tea every night' and daughter writes, 'I make tea on Saturdays' it is all good. You may find that there is some argument about who does what but a little of that is normal. It can be useful in as much as it may allow people to vent emotions at a safe time and also may give you clues as to other work which needs to be done (assessment) but ensure that you manage the situation. Keep it safe. Don't let discussions become too heated. Try to teach compromise and respect. A phrase I often use is, 'I am sure what each of you is saying has truth in it, but now is not the time to get into a big row. Let's agree that you have different experiences/

opinions on the same subject, so you could both write how you see things. That would be a good way of showing both your opinions.'

If this doesn't work, maybe you need to be firmer. Give clear instructions and then offer a distraction/displacement activity: 'Okay folks. Enough! Time to stop. Right – let's have a snack break. Gemma, can you get the cups for me and, Sam, could you please put the biscuits out.'

I have done this activity many times and not had to manage much conflict at all as the families get absorbed in the activity, looking for all the good things to say about each other. The worker is supporting this with positive expectation and distraction if things get negative, so your skills are crucial.

8.   The final step is to put all the hearts in the middle of the table and mix them up. Invite people to pick a heart and read it or describe the picture. Once this is done celebrate with:

   ○ clapping

   ○ making a whoosh sound

   ○ waving hands in the air

   ○ any other action/noise you and the family think of.

One family loved bubbles so for each heart they blew one breath of bubbles from the pot.

If the example of love/care relates to a person in the room, for example, 'I give Anna her bath every night' then you might want to ask Anna to stick that heart onto a door or wall. But if it is a general statement like, 'I make tea' you could just ask the person who wrote it to stick it up or alternatively ask anyone who hasn't had a chance to stick one up yet. It is nice to encourage positive statements from one family member to another by whispering in an ear, 'Maybe you can shout out, "thank you mummy".' This works best if you encourage the young children first as they are less inhibited and eager to please. Once the others see the smiles their positive comments bring, they will often make spontaneous statements.

At the end I praise everyone: 'What a loving family this is' (presuming we have something on the wall to say this – and frankly even half a dozen hearts will do). I am focusing on the positives in a bid to increase that behaviour – if you notice even the small positives you only do good.

If I am confident the family will respond/cope, I suggest a family hug or family high fives or standing in a circle and saying hip hip hooray while lifting our hands in the air. My best outcome will be if they can do a family hug – on their own. The high fives or hand holding can be supported by me. If I am not sure, I will start with the hand holding. If they cope and manage that I will announce, 'Right, high fives now and all together one, two three, go!' If that goes well (I am watching everyone's reaction closely), 'And best for last, let's see you doing a family hug.' If I am in any doubt about this working, if I fear people won't engage or someone would be excluded I won't suggest it.

Practice example

Debbie and her daughter Carly (15) were at loggerheads constantly. There had been longstanding childcare issues. As a younger child Carly had been on the Child Protection Register and now was the subject of a supervision order. Carly had got herself into a place where she believed her mum didn't love her or care about her. Debbie felt that Carly had lost all respect for her and was making statements like, 'Does she really think I don't love her? She must really hate me or she would stop all this behaviour.'

I suggested to Debbie that we do the 'Loving Hearts' exercise, explaining what it was about. Debbie was happy to do it.

Carly was not so easily convinced, 'Do I hell want to do that with you and my mother!' We talked and talked while I drove her to the ice-cream shop (a favourite activity). On reaching the shop we could agree that Carly did want things to change with her mum. Yes, Carly did feel like her mum didn't love her and, crucially, yes, she did trust me. I felt like I was 50 per cent there.

One double chocolate ice-cream purchased; one slightly less unsettled teenager who was almost prepared to smile (she normally only got one scoop) when I added, 'Oh and one chocolate flake with that as this young lady has been doing a lot of hard talking.'

The ice-cream shop manager who was serving us knew us well by now and incidentally knew my job as one of the other number of children I take there had told her, replied, 'I think by the look on your face you need two flakes. Has Audrey been making you work? I'm thinking she's good at that!' This did bring a smile and some more banter from me suggesting they must be working together to make me buy more chocolate. So by the time we got back in the car Carly was relaxed. I started the engine when Carly interrupted me: 'Right, Audrey, don't start on the road home. I'll do the heart thing, okay. I'll do it to keep you quiet and I will see what Mum has got to say for herself. You'll see that I am right. Now, can we no talk and just get the radio on?' (I had not allowed her to have it on on the way there.) I replied, 'You can put the radio on, any station you like, as loud as you like. You are a brave girl and I am proud of you.'

In this sentence I was rewarding her but more importantly I was recognising her fear. I knew there was a fair chance her initial refusal was based on fear. How scary it is to think or feel your mother doesn't love you and then to be able to test that out. Carly had been neglected in her early years by her mum. At that time her mum had not met her needs on any level and she had hard evidence to prove her fears so I knew how brave she was to agree to this activity. We had trust in our relationship. Once again I was reminded of my moral responsibility and I have to admit I was anxious too. When we began the exercise, I needed to get it right.

The old saying, 'Strike while the iron is hot,' came to mind. If I didn't act quickly I was sure Carly would back out.

The next day my appointment diary was full but I was able to rearrange one appointment to allow me to work with Carly and Debbie the following morning. I prepped Debbie by phone before the visit. I explained Carly would find it difficult. I needed Debbie to be 'really adult' and work with me on this one. I reminded her that she was going to need to do more of the work initially. Debbie was not too pleased.

'She's given me dog's abuse and you want me to say all this good stuff!'

'Come on, Debbie, you know you have not given Carly the care she needed in the past. We are in recovery time. You need to be "Mum". You need to help her. She's your wee girl, and I will help you. Okay?'

No response.

'Debbie, she's a teenager. She is going to be difficult most days – that's in a teenager's job description. It's in your job description to care for her, no matter what. Do you care for her, Debbie?'

'Aye, You know that.'

'Right. I need you to show me *and* Carly. Now come on, we can crack this together. Small steps, okay?'

'Aye, okay. When are you coming?'

'11 o'clock this morning.'

'Right.'

'Good. Debbie, I know it is hard. Change is hard. I am proud of you for trying. You have come a long way. You'll be fine. I know you can do this. Okay?'

'Aye, thanks, Audrey. I'll leave the main door open for you.'

And so at 11 o'clock I arrived with all my gear and I confess I was nervous. Over 20 years of practice and sometimes I still get nervous, so if you are starting out in practice, take heart, you are not alone.

This was going to be challenging and I wanted it to work. Carly was up but still in her sleep wear with a blanket wrapped around her. Debbie was dressed, coffee in hand.

'I've no got long for this,' she announced.

'Oh, here she goes,' from Debbie.

Me: 'Hey, guys. Look what I have got,' pulling out the heart shapes, 'I was thinking of you both as I made them. Now you are not going to disappoint me and not use them. It's going to be okay, I promise.'

Debbie: 'Okay, let's do it.'

Me: 'Look, I've written one for you both already. It says,
         "Debbie shows her love for Carly by wanting Carly
         home each night by 10.30pm" and "Carly shows her
         love for Debbie by coming home every night even if
         she doesn't quite manage to be in by 10.30pm."'

They both agreed with this and smiled.

To my utter relief both Debbie and Carly took the offered
hearts and wrote diligently on them. I sat beside Carly for the
first 20 minutes or so whispering encouragement: 'Hey, good
thinking', 'Well done you for thinking of that', 'Good lass'.

I made eye contact with Debbie, smiling reassuringly.
Occasionally she would hold a heart up for me to read and I
would give her a thumbs up or nod and smile. In this way I was
supporting both.

Before they began to flag I stopped the exercise. Better to
stop when they still had something to write. It leaves a sense of
the exercise being easy – non-stressful, and creates optimism.

Some of the things Carly and Debbie wrote were:

'I make your tea and buy your clothes and food and stuff.'

'I love you, Carly, more than my own life.'

'I don't want you to drink [alcohol] 'cause I love you.'

'I shout at you to get back home because I love you and
don't want anything bad to happen.'

'I made mistakes when I was your age and because I love
you I don't want you to do the bad stuff I did.'

'I make your breakfast because I love you.'

'I pick up my towel like you always tell me to do because I
love you.'

'I love you, Mum, but I want to be with my friends. It's
embarrassing to come home by 10.30pm.'

'I don't want you to go out with Jack, Mum, because I don't
like the way he treats you.'

'I smoke, that's my business but just because I don't listen to you doesn't mean I don't love you.'

'I'm doing this because I want you to know I love you.'

They managed a mother and daughter hug and both were happy at the end. This had cleared the air. There was obviously more work to do and within 48 hours they had fallen out again but they had their hearts stuck to the wall and I was pleased when Debbie told me she had referred Carly to them. I knew I had lots more work to do, but was relieved the exercise had worked and we had made a positive start.

XVI. Memory Bank
Purpose

- This is really a way of helping a family reflect on their experiences and identify resilience. Remembering and reflecting on the past can help a family to understand their strengths as well as their vulnerabilities and help them to consider how to deal with their current circumstances.

- This exercise can also be done with one person.

What you need

- Something to hold the items – this is the Bank. This can be a shoebox which can be decorated with coloured paper and stickers etc. Or maybe you can buy a container/box to be the Bank and the family can decorate it with paint, pens and whatever is to hand to make it their own. I have also made a 'tree' using a branch (which you may want to paint) placed in a jar or big flower pot and weighed down with stones to secure it. This would make a Memory Tree. Memories are then written on labels and tied to the branch. I have also used soft toys made into pyjama cases and the pictures/writing of memories goes into the 'tummy'. The key is that the Bank has to be claimed by the family as a special object and the making of the Memory Bank may be one of the memories it might contain.

- You will also need luggage labels (made of cardboard) to write the memories on. If you have made a tree, these can be tied on.

- A4 paper, perhaps coloured, to write on and post into the container/Bank. This is the best option when there are young children in the family as they can draw their memories (and the adult could maybe write on the back what the memory is). Young children need space to draw. A4 is a relatively small piece of paper if you are under 5 years or the child's development is in line with pre-school ability as hand–eye coordination and fine motor skills mean more space is needed to enjoy drawing.

- Good quality felt tip pens, in good working order (nothing is more frustrating than ink drying out or the nib breaking as a child concentrates hard to commit thought to paper).

- I prefer to work at a table (I bring my own folding picnic table as many of the families I visit don't have a table).

- I often work with families in their own home but you make your own judgement. A room in the office or community centre can work well if this supports concentration and focus and means fewer interruptions from dogs, neighbours, etc.

- Some drinks and snacks. I like to provide fresh fruit juice or water and pour this into colourful plastic cups I bring with me. I also try to offer healthy snacks like raisins or fruit. This provides a sense of occasion which children love and appreciate. I also want to model good parenting behaviour. Providing a snack is a nurturing activity and attends to children's physical wellbeing, and the sharing of food can promote conversation.

- It is always good to provide new tastes. I offered a parent a date once. They politely but firmly refused, 'I don't eat those shrivelled-up things.' However, the child of 2 had no such qualms and happily enjoyed the dates as did the 4-year-old. Next week I cut the dates into four and asked the parent if they would like to try it. 'It's very sweet and sticky and look, the children love them.' I then took and ate a piece myself. The parent tried it and liked it and asked what it was. When I told her it was a date she raised her eyebrows but asked, 'Where do you get them?' The following week the child had taken a date to her nursery teacher to try.

What to do

1. First of all make the Memory Bank. As I said earlier it needs to be claimed by the family as their special object so if they like a lot of bling you might provide glitter, acrylic gems and gold and silver paper and so on to use for decoration. If they love dogs maybe you could provide dog stickers. But do give as much choice as you can. While decorating the memory box begin to talk about your memories of the family.

   'I remember the first day I met you…'

   'Do you remember the day I brought the paints and we did family painting?'

   'Can you remember the first day I visited? What do you remember?'

   'I can see a photo over there. What can you tell me about that?'

   'Can you think of a worst and best memory since I last visited?'

   Try to generate discussion and allow time for memories to just tumble out. If people are struggling, point out that we have made memories today. 'I remember when I arrived…who can remember something from today?'

2. At this point I would be jotting down a few notes to guide me in the next part of the process.

3. Meanwhile the focus is on decorating the box/tree etc. and creating a sense of fun but also respect. I will expect and insist that people listen to each other.

4. Once the Bank is decorated, you want to help get those memories on paper. They can be written, drawn (with the adult writing a few words) or dictated to the worker who writes them down, remembering to read it back to check it is correct.

5. Sometimes one person will have a memory but another person in recalling the same event will have a different recollection of it. Now before a family argument sets off, remind everybody that is quite normal. It is just that people have different roles in life and therefore memories of events are different but each equally important. It is possible that there is some distortion of the truth but in most situations this will not be the case. In situations where it is the case, it will not be new behaviour. I find the best way to deal with this is to make a memory string: everyone remembers their own personal memory of the event and then we string them together, so when the memory is pulled out of the Bank, all versions are there.

6. It is okay and indeed should be encouraged, to include both good and bad memories. The collection can take time and should not be rushed. You may want to do it over two sessions. As we are making memories all the time the activity should never really stop.

7. At mid point, offer the snack/nurture activity. Once you have a good collection of memories, ask the family's permission to keep the Memory Bank for a short while (I would suggest no longer than a week). Explain that you won't open it, just keep it safe. The next time you visit there will be a great ceremony of the opening of the Memory Bank.

Next visit

1. Make it special. I bring lots of small bottles of bubbles that will be blown before a memory is picked out of the box or after one is read and before the next. Sometimes I have a cake and soft drink as it is a special occasion after all. I might wear my storytelling clock (a velvet cloth clock). We might sprinkle a little glitter on everyone's head to help have a magical time and everyone will have to do a 'drum roll' (tapping hands on knees) when a memory

is pulled out. We will take turns in pulling a memory out and sharing it, that is, reading aloud or showing (appropriate help given to non-confident readers). Memories good, bad, powerful, silly are all valued and discussed.

'Hey, what would you do if that happened again?'

'You smiled a lot when you heard that. Did it make you happy? Yes! Could you remember that next time you feel sad?'

'Ah, part of that memory was about giving hugs. Do you like hugs? You do! Okay, can you choose someone to give a big hug to now?'

'Could we have a big, huge, massive, best-ever family hug?'

'Okay, sounds like that was a sad memory. It is hard when people die and okay to be sad then and now. If you need to cry that's okay [*pause*]. Can you think of any other Granny memories? You can? Let's get them down and add them to the Bank.'

2. Once the memories are shared reflect on how it felt and see if anyone has memories to add: 'Did anybody learn anything? I always learn something! Today I learned that you are a family like lots of other families who have had quite a hard time but you are strong (or stronger now) and you've had good times too. I wonder if we could plan another activity so we can add that to the Memory Bank.'

3. Encourage the family to keep adding memories, good or bad and to keep reviewing them. Initially you will most likely need to prompt and support this but it is worth it. One parent said, 'It's so easy to forget the good bits and just get depressed thinking of all the stuff that goes wrong and then I read the memory about the barbecue at the Centre and think, well it's no all bad.' Another child said, 'I like the Memory Bank 'cause I know which bit of paper I wrote my memory about Dad on. So if I want to talk about him I just cheat and pull that bit of paper out and then I can talk about him and it's not like I made Mum talk about Dad 'cause really the Memory Bank did.' A younger child said, 'I like the box 'cause it's sparkly and I get to draw and Mum smiles.'

Practice examples

I used this exercise with a family where there had been sustained domestic abuse. The father now lived away from the home but returned fairly often and in effect continued to cause fear and alarm. The mother and children made a Memory Bank and one of the children (9 years old) wrote the following: 'I remember that Dad put his hands around Mum's neck and I punched him in the back but he didn't stop and he broke Mum's phone so I couldn't do the number [for the police] and I don't like seeing Dad hurting my Mum he's not to do that 'cause hurting is bad and he needs to stay at his flat and not come here and make Mum and me cry.'

In reviewing this memory, the child who was not a confident reader, asked me to read it out but stood beside me and looked directly at her mum as it was read. Trudy found it very moving to hear Mary's words and said she was sorry and hugged her. Mary said very firmly, 'It's not your fault, it's Dad.'

In a separate session with me, Trudy reflected on Mary's words and this provided her with the strength to make the decision to move house in an attempt to permanently separate from her abusive partner. I suggested that she write a letter to Mary for when she was an adult about the memory of this experience. In the present, she acknowledged Mary's views and told her that the family would move house. The reason I requested she write now to the adult Mary was:

1. Future investment in the mother/daughter relationship. Even if the plan to separate didn't work Mary would know her mum had listened to her and acted on her worries.

2. To help Trudy to consolidate her plan and reflect on the process.

Working with another family and reviewing their Memory Bank which was full of loss and change, we were able to acknowledge how much they had come through. I gave information about 'normal reactions' to loss and the mother and oldest child were able to identify themselves as 'doing okay, I suppose. We have coped with a hell of a lot.' I helped them to begin to view themselves as survivors who had acquired many skills and were also the experts on themselves, and how they had managed to cope. In doing this they became less critical and more positive. I also challenged them to make happy memories to add to the Bank. I emphasised they did not have to be big events but 'little happies' are just as valuable. I suggested that my little happies were things like 'I saw a rainbow today' or 'My cat enjoyed chasing a butterfly and looked very cute.'

I asked, could they think of any happies?

Mum came up with:

'I thought I had run out of coffee but I hadn't.'

'My friend had a baby.'

'I had enough money to buy fags.'

The teenage girl came up with:

'I won at Candy Crush.'

'My pal lent me her hair straighteners.'

'Mum and I have no argued today.'

In recognising small positives in life people can become more positive about themselves and in turn be enabled to feel more in control and take more responsibility. Once you feel that you can have a positive influence on your own circumstances, even if that is small, improved mental health should follow. I should add that I am not suggesting that when someone has a diagnosed mental health problem such as depression, that simply changing the way you think will cure it. However, people who are experiencing low mood or are just overwhelmed by difficulties can and do improve their outlook on life by positive self-talk and this is what I am referring to.

XVII. The Detective and the Sniffer Dog

Purpose

- To create an opportunity for family members to talk about emotions and to provide an opportunity for assessing family dynamics; emotional literacy; speech and language; and ability to empathise.

- It also gives the worker an opportunity to model parenting skills including offering praise and encouragement.

What you need

- A flipchart and stand (A3 size paper).

- Big felt tip pens in working order.

- A dog hand puppet (or a dog soft toy would do).

- Dog-bone shapes made out of cardboard.

Preparation before the session

Prepare the flipchart by drawing the detective and his dog. (Draw your own or use the template in Appendix V, adding a dog. If the family you are working with have a pet dog, a quick internet search will help you to make a simple line drawing of that breed. Otherwise, choose a suitable cartoon drawing of a dog to copy, ensuring you are not breaching copyright.) We need two identical pictures per session. Cut out enough bone shapes allowing four for each person per session.

What to do

This activity is better if it is done away from the family home; in my case I usually do it in the office, to make sure there are no distractions such as television, computer games or pets so I can give my full concentration to the family.

1. Once you have welcomed the family and everyone is sitting down around the flipchart (ensuring there is space for family members to walk up to the chart and write on it), introduce the detective enthusiastically. Tell the family that he (or she) is going to do

some detective work about the family. Today he wants to find out how people in this family show they are happy, sad, angry, jealous, upset and so on.

2. Pick two emotions to have a trial run for the family. I usually pick 'happy' and 'angry' as they are feelings familiar to most, starting with happy as it is usually a safe emotion. It helps the family become comfortable with the activity.

3. 'So, let's help him.' At this point I give out pens, letting people choose a colour. Each person should have a different colour.

4. 'If the detective and his sniffer dog came to visit your home one day, how would they know you were happy? What would you be doing that would show you were happy?' Each person then gets a turn to write on the chart. Younger children can draw a picture if they can't or don't wish to write and you can write the words they use under it. Everyone should write at least one thing or more if they wish.

5. When all have had their turn, offer praise – for example for completing the task, for working well together, for all the different ways they show they are happy and for giving it careful thought.

6. It is now the turn of the facilitator to encourage discussion. 'So, Dad, the detective and his sniffer dog would know you are happy because you are smiling! Has anyone else written smiling? Yes! Morag has. Can anyone else tell me what other things Dad and Morag do when they are happy?' You are now asking family members to give feedback on each other's behaviour. Happy is usually a safe emotion to begin with as most happy behaviour is positive and therefore it is easier to give feedback. It helps the family to get used to doing this kind of work. To avoid anyone feeling 'got at' try to ask for feedback on two family members at a time, say a parent and a child. This helps defuse any tensions caused by one person feeling they are being targeted. It is especially relevant in families where negative behaviour is more of an issue.

7. I then add with my own pen the comments other people make under each individual's statement of what they do when they

are happy, attributing the comment to the person who made it. For example, 'Dad says Morag walks round the house with a big grin on her face.' It is important all the comments go up, even if the subject is protesting it is not true, as the aim is to help people reflect on behaviour and take responsibility. This includes the parents who will often receive very honest and blunt feedback from the children. I may sometimes soften comments, for example if Dad says Morag walks around with a big silly grin on her face I may change it to a big grin. If the subject is very upset by the feedback I may add, 'But Morag says this is not true, she just smiles.'

8. When you have finished the trial run, offer praise and reward to the participating members. I have a small bag of sweets, stickers etc. that they can dip into and pick out an item. This is important as it is often emotionally hard to do this work. Make it fun and emphasise the achievement. You want the experience to end on a positive for Dad and Morag and you want the other members to be willing to participate when it comes to them.

9. You can now proceed with the other family members in the same way. By the time you finish, you will have recorded on the picture a great deal of information about how the family works.

10. You can now repeat the above activity for 'angry'. You may only get through two emotions in one session. It depends on how talkative your family is, their concentration levels and the amount of emotion expressed. You will have to judge when to stop. I tend to have a one-hour slot but will stop sooner if I need to and also I try to build in flexibility to go on another 20 mins or so if I feel that is best.

Optional activity
This part is optional but it is fun. You could use it at the start of Session 2 as a warm-up and a way of recapping work done in Session 1. Or it could be used at the end of a session as a way to end on a lighter note.

Give everyone a cardboard bone and ask them to write on the bone what makes them happy. This should be kept secret. Then ask the family to leave the room while you hide them. When they return and are seated again, hand the dog puppet to the youngest in the room and ask them to sniff out a bone and bring it back to you. We read it aloud together and then the person has to guess who wrote it. If they are right, we clap and the bone is returned to the owner with a hug or paw-shake from the puppet. This creates an opportunity for affection and warmth to be shared and asking the dog puppet to do it creates safety in families where demonstrations of affection are rare or where family members are uncomfortable with touch. In families comfortable with showing affection, a spontaneous hug will sometimes follow after the dog has offered its hug.

If the guess is incorrect (this happens a lot), keeping the tone light and fun, ask who owns the bone. This is then returned in the same way.

The aim is to increase the family's understanding of its members and increase or reinforce emotional literacy. We should be demonstrating and encouraging acceptance and empathy. It gives us an opportunity to assess individual speech and language skills, emotional development and literacy, and gives an understanding of family dynamics and parenting skills.

Now repeat the activity using 'anger'. I would hope that by this time the family are more relaxed and confident and ready to look at more sensitive issues. It is a good idea to give two bones to each person for this. On the first, ask each person to write down what makes them angry and on the second what they do to help them calm down.

I usually assign an hour to each session. If it is any longer I will have a break and offer a small snack and drink. When doing this activity, it goes without saying that the more family members there are the longer it will take. If there are children under 8 years in the family, I will provide toys or paper and crayons for when they get restless but I ask them to play in front of the flipchart in the middle of the circle to keep them central to the activity. They are encouraged to chip in and take their own turn when it comes. Some parents may need help in accepting this way of working, feeling their child should conform to the rules of the game. Sitting in a chair for an hour is too much to expect of young children and this can give you an opportunity to model appropriate parenting.

Practice example
Family

Mum – Laura

Dad – Bert

David (15)

Stuart (13)

Poppy (9)

Mark (8)

Danny (7)

The children in this reconstituted family were being monitored under child protection procedures in relation to sexual abuse by Laura's previous partner. There were also concerns about Bert's offending history which included significant acts of violence in the community.

Both Laura and Bert said they found David and Stuart's behaviour particularly difficult to cope with (non-compliance with family rules; failing to come home on time; non-attendance at school and disruption when they did attend). David said he wanted Bert to leave the home as he was not his dad. Stuart liked Bert but said he never had enough time with him. Poppy was looking forward to a promised puppy after they moved house. Mark and Danny were less responsive about their mum living with Bert but did say they didn't like the new, larger house they had moved into. They wanted to go home. Danny seemed sad and somewhat lost. Mark was oppositional and angry but still fairly compliant with adults.

I realised we had an awful lot of emotions to look at. Also, I noticed they were rarely together as a family group. Most significantly there seemed to be a lot of misunderstanding of how each other felt and some fairly harsh and unkind responses to each other.

My aim was to increase the family's emotional literacy (I had noticed the children struggled to find words to describe emotions), encourage empathy, support communication about emotions and assess family dynamics.

So I decided to use this activity. As it was a big family I split the session into two on consecutive days; otherwise it would have been too long. I concentrated on the emotion 'happy' one day and 'angry' the other. The sessions took place in the office.

The happy session went well, with a lot of laughter. I had briefed the parents beforehand to watch out for good behaviour and reward it by giving a treat from the bag and also encouraged parents to reward with positive words and attention. It is important to find ways to help parents do this as it is common to find a lack of this in families. Where there is a lack or warmth and praise children's emotional needs are not met and parents are disempowered in terms of behaviour management. I only provide two sweets per child to model that a sweet and/or sticker should be the special treat and verbal praise should be the norm. I asked the parents to catch the children when they were being good and give 100 per cent attention to the child when handing over the treat. I also praised the parents when they demonstrated good parenting.

The family left the session in good humour. The next day the session on anger proved to be a significant one for the family. When they arrived I sensed a low mood and it transpired there had been an argument which was still festering. In order to release the tension before attempting the activity, I used the only thing I had to hand which was play dough and got the family to thump and bang it into any shape they fancied. This broke the tension and produced some laughter, so we could begin.

The family proved to be motivated and quickly added to the picture on the flipchart the many things they did to show they were angry. Swear, shout, punch the wall, look grumpy, bang the pots around as I cook, go to my room and not talk to anyone, drink, don't come home on time, break my dolls.

Some of these brought new understanding. Mum said to Poppy, 'Darling, I didn't know you broke your dolls because you were angry. I just thought you were being bad. Why are you angry?' Poppy replied that she didn't always know but sometimes it was because she was bullied in school. Mum was shocked and asked why she didn't tell her. Poppy shrugged and her brother chipped in to say that he got detention because he hit the girl who was bullying his sister.

A conversation around bullying and the children's experience took place and it led to David saying he thought Bert bullied his mum and that was why he didn't want them to live together and why he stayed out late. This shocked Bert who was visibly upset and Laura tried to reassure David. With the parents' agreement I said this was something we could explore in 'Laura and Bert time' and I made an appointment to do this at the end of the session.

The hiding-the-bones session revealed that family members had coping or calming techniques that others were unaware of. Poppy stated she liked to go to her granny's house when angry or upset because she liked cuddling the cat. Laura had not understood this before and had always refused Poppy's spontaneous requests to go to Granny as it was some distance away and not planned.

Danny was able to say that at school he was given a ball to kick if he got angry. Bert realised he removed Danny's football as a sanction at home and as a result Danny kicked in the doors which led to further sanctions.

Laura also revealed that her coping mechanism was to cook a special meal when angry or upset and so when the children or Bert declined to eat it, an already emotional Laura over-reacted by swearing and shouting. Bert said, laughing, that in future he would eat anything she put down for him.

The session ended in good humour. On the following home visits I concentrated on individual work with the children and time with Bert and Laura, looking at behaviour management, before returning to do further sessions with the detective and his dog.

This activity increased the parents' and children's understanding of each other and opened up communication around emotion and behaviour. In the following home visits we were able to refer back to the activity and use it as a template in discussion with the parents to encourage them to look at why the children were behaving the way they were. For example, 'Remember, Bert, you discovered that removing the football was removing a coping mechanism that Danny had learned to use to deal with his anger. Could something similar be happening in the situation you have just described?'

I noted as well that Laura in particular became more able to use verbal praise and her use of sanctions became more appropriate. The family continued to require significant support and monitoring, both of which they had stated they did not want. They were able to recognise the benefits of this kind of work and remained engaged.

XVIII. Ripple Stones
Purpose

- A visual demonstration of how one person's actions can impact on others.

What you need

- Small flat pebbles of different shapes and colours (these can be bought from a garden centre if you don't have a natural source).

- A basin full of water.

- A towel or newspaper to place under the basin to protect the floor from splashes of water.

What to do

1. Sit or stand the family around the basin.

2. Give everyone a pebble. Try to have pebbles of different colours and shapes or you could use acrylic marker for each person to mark their own stone.

3. Ask the first person to plop (notice I didn't say throw) their stone into the water.

   ○ Enjoy the moment.

   ○ Look what happens.

   ○ Can you see the ripples?

   ○ Did the colour of the stone change once it entered the water?

  ○ Did you hear it plop?

4. Invite the others to plop their stones in.

  ○ Where did they land?

  ○ Had the first ripples stopped before the next stone added ripples? Is the sound different now there are more stones in the water?

5. Now everyone has to rescue their stones from the basin. Explain you are now going to pretend the stones are family members and the bowl is the house.

6. Invite an adult to plop their stone into the water. Once the ripples have stopped you might say something to the effect of:

    'So Mum is at home, the house is quiet. What are you doing, Mum?'

    Mum: 'Reading the paper and watching TV.'

    'Oh, it's 4.15 and so the children come home from school. Okay, everyone who goes to school plop your stones in.'

7. Observe how all the ripples collide and explain that that is like everyone trying to tell Mum all at once about their day until eventually the water settles again.

8. Practise this and encourage the family to tell you about family life when people's actions impact on others.

Practice example

I did this activity with a family of three – a mother and two children; a boy of 10 and a girl of 5 years. There had been domestic abuse and the father was at this point excluded from the family home and had no contact with the children. The children had witnessed him seriously assaulting their mother. Mum and Dad continued in a relationship, reportedly seeing each other when the children were in school. Mum said she wanted Dad to return home and I think the children were aware of this. My purpose in doing this exercise was aimed at Mum who had limited self-awareness but also aimed at the

10-year-old boy to try to help him to see that his angry and aggressive behaviour towards his mum did have an impact.

I wanted to do this in a very gentle way which did not focus on him at all, but rather was a general lesson. The little girl was too young to see the analogy but I knew she would enjoy the water play. However, I was pleased when Matt used this activity to show us his observation of what happened when Dad was around.

We had gone through the explaining part and the first story had been around Mum shouting for the children to come in for tea. Hope, aged 5, was telling us her story which was essentially about feeding the ducks. I had gently advised Mum and Matt to listen though they didn't feel that Hope was playing the game properly and were trying to correct her. I told them Hope was very young and she just needed to join in her way. Hope was enjoying the water play and in fact was the centre of attention which was a good boost to her self-esteem.

Matt, who struggles to take turns and listen, was desperate for his own turn and on reflection maybe had increased energy as a stress response because he was about to convey a big message.

'I'm gonna tell you a true and mega story,' he announced just as soon as Hope finished. He dived in and took all the stones out and then said, 'Right, you've all got to put stones in now all at once.'

Mum and Hope complied. Matt left the kitchen, heading towards the back door saying, 'Wait there. I have to get something.'

He came back very quickly with a very large stone from the back garden. I was slightly worried. I got an anxious look from Mum who was about to protest. I motioned her to keep silent and said, 'It's Matt's turn, respect that,' but I was really holding on to my nerve. My sense was that Matt had something urgent and important to tell us. Although I was worried that the stone was too big, the social worker in me was convinced I needed to go with it. I pulled Hope back a bit and at that moment Matt dropped the stone in the basin and shouted, 'And that's what happens when Dad comes!', looking directly at Mum.

Mum looked shocked and tears sprang in her eyes. 'You are right, son.' They had a hug while I cleared up the watery mess!

Chapter 12

Simple Ideas to Increase Parent/Child Proximity and Positive Touch

Many, if not most, of the parents I work with have trauma in their past. For a good majority this can leave them in a position where positive parenting does not come easily and in particular they will need support to help bond with the child so the child can build healthy attachments. Most of these parents do want their children's experience to be better than their own, but achieving this can be very challenging. Improving material circumstances is easier compared to making changes in emotional care if you have limited emotional resources to draw on yourself. Sometimes taught activities to use with children can help. Essentially you are working on improving attachment. You will notice that these activities are very simple. Most parents play instinctively with their children, but if your needs were not met in your own childhood, you may need to be taught.

1. Family Hat
Purpose

- Building a child's self-esteem.

- Creating an opportunity for parent/child bonding.

- Teaching a parent an activity to enhance their bonding and ability to give positive feedback to the child.

What you need

- An old hat that the family can decorate (this can be an activity in itself).
- A sheet or blanket.
- Singing/chanting voice.
- Big smile and sense of fun.

What to do

1. Place the hat on the child's head and to the tune of 'The sun has got his hat on' sing, '[Child's name] has got her hat on, hip, hip, hip, hooray. [Child's name] has got her hat on and she is coming out to play.'

2. The parent takes the child to walk around the room or sits the child on their knee and bounces them, singing, '[Child's name] has got her hat on, hip, hip, hip, hooray. [Child's name] has got her hat on and we love her every day', followed by a big cuddle.

2. Family Den
Purpose

- Creating opportunities for positive physical contact.
- Supporting nurturing play.
- Creating opportunities to have fun.

What you need

- A sheet or rug.
- Cushions or a pillow.

What to do

1. Make a family den. A sheet spread across two chairs perhaps or pull the sofa forward and put lots of pillows behind it making

enough space for adult and child to cuddle up in. Perhaps put a favourite teddy in there and a book.

2. You can encourage the family to chant, 'We are in our family den. Hip, hip, hip, hooray. We are in our family den, let's cuddle up today.'

3. As the worker who is supporting this activity you are going to help Mum or Dad feel comfortable playing. You might make statements like:

    ○ 'Good cuddling, Mum.'

    ○ 'Nice eye contact.'

    ○ 'Lovely voice.'

    ○ 'Maybe try a rub on the head?!'

    In addition to the above, joining in with the play using a big puppet or teddy/doll as your child, you can model behaviour for Mum and Dad.

3. Make Your Own Bubbles
Purpose

-   To provide a nurturing and fun experience.

-   To create proximity between parent and child.

What you need

-   A sink/wash basin with water.

-   A bar of soap.

-   Two towels (one of them for the floor!).

-   Mirror above the washbasin.

What to do

Sometimes the best way to teach a parent how to do this and the value in it, is to do it yourself with the child (you should know the child well and have established trust) while they watch. People tend to assume you would do this with a preschooler but older children often love it, especially those who have not had enough positive early-years experiences.

1. Run warm water into the basin while you are standing behind the child.

2. Point out the steam rising, water splashing etc. and make fun comments and noises.

3. Once you have a little water in the sink (enough to cover the hand when laid flat), give the child the soap and ask them to try and make lots of bubbles. Ask permission to help and, if given, put your hands on theirs.

4. Continue to play with the soap, making bubbles and gently touching the child's hands. Comment on what you see and feel and try making bubbles as many different ways as you can.

5. Use the mirror if there is one to increase communication. Lots of smiles and exaggerated expressions. Very satisfying and fun.

Children can spend hours doing this. It is usually the adult who gets fed up first. As the worker I will only do it for a few minutes to demonstrate to the parent what to do – not just how to make the bubbles but how to engage the child. Once I judge that the parent is engaged in the activity – that is, they are interested and want to join in – then I will announce, 'Right, Mummy's turn' and change places, becoming the observer. Some parents need little support after this point but many need a significant level of support. The child sometimes needs reassurance, if there is a lack of trust and positive expectation in the parent/child relationship. Some parents also need to know that they are doing it right. You have to use your experience to judge how much to say. I have had children who take their hands out of the water and move away when it is Mummy's turn. Clearly in the context of other concerns this can be a significant indicator of how uncomfortable the child feels. Be careful not to make assumptions. This kind of reaction will be noted and will add to the assessment but one incident like this does not make an assessment. It may be that the child was ready to stop play anyway.

On a practical level, encourage Mum to carry on. This may be easier said than done, but try to use humour and reassurance. 'It's okay, maybe [child] just wants a break but at least you have the whole sink to yourself now!'

Out of earshot of the child tell Mum to carry on and see if the child will return. Many times the child will gravitate back to the adults who are having fun. If they do, just include them with no fuss. If the child doesn't return after some time change places with Mum ('My turn now!') and see if that brings the child back. If they do, this may be an indicator that *on that day* there is an issue with them not wanting to play *in this way* with the parent. It's worth asking the child very gently about this and also asking the parent. Remain curious; don't assume negatives.

If the child doesn't come back to play with you, continue in your own play for five to 10 minutes while talking to the parent. The reason for this is you want to ensure the child has enough opportunity to join in again. It's their activity and if they were having fun with you and then *you* instigated change by inviting Mum to play with them, then in their eyes you have spoiled their fun and been unfair so you have a duty to try to make amends.

But the other potential issue is that there is a power struggle between parent and child and the child has disengaged to assert their power. It is not good for children to feel they are in charge of the adults or can dictate the agenda any time they want (it is quite appropriate sometimes) so by not stopping immediately they disengage, you remain in control.

4. Hand Cream and/or Nail Polish
Purpose

- To create a nurturing experience.
- To create an opportunity for positive interaction between parent and child.

What you need

- Hand cream.
- Nail polish and remover.

What to do

This activity really doesn't need any instructions and occurs regularly in children's centres. The reason I am including it is because I know the positive impact it can have. For some young people, close physical contact has been a frightening or hurtful experience and for others they haven't experienced enough loving touches. This can lead to much potentially harmful behaviour as young people seek to meet this need in dysfunctional ways.

This activity does require trust and so we can demonstrate our trust in them by allowing the young person to do our nails first and the same can be said of the parent/child relationship.

> **Practice example**
>
> Katrina was nearly 16 and she and her mum Fiona were always at loggerheads. But they both liked fashion. A pattern was developing that each time I visited they both wanted to tell me at once how awful the other was. The younger three girls meanwhile also vied for my attention.
>
> One day I brought hand cream and nail polish with me. I introduced this as an activity for Katrina and Fiona only while I worked with the younger children. Both were a bit taken aback but were keen to do their nails and enjoyed helping each other. They talked as they worked together and I was pleased to hear Katrina asking Mum's permission to go to a party in a calm and respectful way.
>
> At the end of the visit I reflected this back to them which brought laughter and acknowledgment. I 'prescribed' hand cream and nail polish once a week after the little ones were in bed. Both followed this strictly. If there were excuses, 'I'm tired' or 'I can't be bothered', they would remind each other that Audrey would ask and this was enough for them to do the activity. Their relationship improved overall and over time.
>
> Katrina told me, 'When mum did my nails I felt like she loved me again, like I mattered. It was good. We sat together like I was small again and I felt kinda safe. Now I am older I do her hair and she gave me a home perm. I guess we feel closer when we do that stuff.'

5. Positive Strokes
Purpose

- To create opportunities for parent and child to share positive and appropriate touch.

What you need

- Yourself and a big doll or teddy.
- A warm and comfortable place.

What to do

1. Explain to the parent in advance why positive touch is important – its role in the parent and child bonding process. Acknowledge that this doesn't come naturally to everybody and not everybody finds it easy to do. A lot of the adults we work with will have had trauma in childhood and this will mean that many as a result have developed damaged, or insecure, attachments which can lead to them feeling stressed when it comes to touch. Sometimes the simple acknowledgement of this in a generalised way can free them up to talk openly about this.

2. Tell the parent that an easy way to include this in daily life is to use songs/rhymes with actions.

3. With the teddy bear, demonstrate this to the parent. Sitting with the teddy bear on your knee where the parent can see your actions, sing or say the rhyme while doing the actions. The rhyme goes:

    > The baby in the cradle goes rock, rock, rock. [gentle movements back and forth across the back]
    >
    > The clock in the kitchen goes tick, tick, tock. [Tap fingers on shoulders.]
    >
    > The rain on the window goes pit, pit, pat. [Use your fingers to drum on the back like raindrops falling.]
    >
    > Here comes the sun! [Soft circular movement on the back.]
    >
    > So we all clap, clap, clap. [Clap hands.]
    >
    > And let's have a cuddle after that. [Cuddle child.]

4. As you sing the rhyme demonstrate the hand movements: gentle hand movements across the back; gentle taps on the shoulders; gentle drumming on the back for rain and a soft circular movement across the back for the sun. Help the teddy to clap hands and have a big cuddle at the end.

5. Next invite the parent to do it with the child while you do it again with the bear.

6. In terms of how you involve the child, do give this a bit of thought. For most parents and children this is really straightforward. Children want to have the adults' time and attention and require little more than a playful invitation to come and play. But once I misjudged a parent and didn't describe how to invite the child to join in, as the practice example shows.

Practice example

When I invited Mum to learn a new song-and-touch game with her 3-year-old, the parent said, 'Get your arse over here 'til I do something to your back.' The little boy looked at Mum who was almost smiling and very cautiously went slowly towards her. I started to smile and say that it was all right, we were going to play a game and sing a song and that I would do it with teddy and Mum would do it with him. To my surprise, James took the teddy and gave it to Mum and said, 'Mummy do it to Teddy and you do it to me.'

Mum did not comprehend the significance of this request and quite happily took the bear and James came to me. We sang the song with the actions and James loved it. After repeating it I said quietly to him, 'Your turn to go to Mummy. What do you think?' He ran to Mum with a big smile, pulled the bear off her knee and threw it at me. He firmly planted himself on Mum's knee and we did the activity at least five more times, James responding with an infectious enthusiasm.

At the next visit, I talked it through with Mum, telling her how well she had done, praising her when she told me she had done it again after I left and on numerous occasions since. Almost to myself, I then wondered aloud why James wanted to do it with me first. Mum replied that James would 'likely be worried that I would clout [hit] him one.'

This opened up a discussion around physical chastisement and trust. I assessed the level of the punishment from what she described and felt this was over-chastisement and advised against it. The concerns up to that point had been around neglect but in this conversation it became evident that issues of over-chastisement needed to be addressed.

If you want to find other activities for babies and toddlers, you can try the local library or go to a children's nursery and talk to staff about what games and songs young children enjoy. Positive touch is so important for brain development in a young child that we cannot stress this enough and many of our parents need help with this, often due to their own neglect in childhood.

Chapter 13

Behaviour

Modelling behaviour

Social workers getting alongside clients and doing simple tasks with them seems to have fallen out of favour over the years. It may be that the job became so overloaded with administrative tasks that it became increasingly difficult to make time, but we have also heard other reasons such as not encouraging dependency. This was a firmly held belief for a while. 'How can they be adequate parents if they can't even remember appointments?' Advances in neuroscience have helped us better understand the effect of chronic stress and alcohol or drug misuse on the brain. Memory is often affected and parents have to learn new methods of recall. Initially this requires constant prompting until the brain rewires.

There has also been a sense that some felt this type of work was more suited to support workers, something we would disagree with as not only is it an invaluable assessment tool but also it is a powerful way of building relationships. Fortunately it is coming back in, with a new name, pedagogy. We think we have been practising this way for years, but calling it 'modelling behaviour'. How else are children and their parents to learn the basic social skills and cultural norms if they have been marginalised for years – sometimes for generations – or been brought up in abject neglect? Terse directives such as 'You have to show you can parent' or 'You need to clean up your house' can render these parents immobile with anxiety and confusion. To give these directions without offering support, care and an opportunity to learn how to meet these requests is only setting up parents to fail. If they cannot achieve the changes requested in time to meet the child's developmental needs then it is fairer and more honest to acknowledge this and decisions will be made with that in mind. Modelling behaviour can also be fun. Having fun produces dopamine which helps reduce stress. Fun can make us laugh – therapy in itself. It also strengthens relationships with the worker and other family members. We will give examples in this chapter but the opportunities are endless.

Practice example
The birthday cake

Annie was going to be 9 years old. She was from a travelling family who had recently settled in a home because of the ill health of a parent. There were concerns about neglect, emotional abuse and non-attendance at school but the family were very resistant to working with outside agencies and could be hostile and even aggressive and threatening. There were three adults in the house and it took a long time and a lot of patience, persistence and creative working for me to get into the home and work on a regular basis with Annie and her family.

About a year into my work with them, Annie was able to relax with me, she was attending school regularly, her physical care had improved and she was attending the health services when required. Now we just had to focus on the hardest part – the emotional care.

Annie presented me with the perfect opportunity to begin this. I was doing some individual work with her – making fruit sculptures – when we had this conversation.

'Audrey, it's my birthday soon.'

'Yes, I know. Don't worry I haven't forgotten,' I replied, smiling.

'I'm getting a scooter. A red one.'

'You are lucky. That's a big present. What do you do in your family when someone has a birthday?'

'What do you mean?'

'Well, does the birthday person get a card, or a special meal or a cake?'

'I might get a card from my nana with money in it. But I have never had a cake. I've always wanted one but I have never got one.' Annie then talked about feeling different when friends at school brought birthday cake in to share.

'Well, not every family has birthday cake but if you could have one what would it be like?'

'It would be chocolate and it would be the shape of a cat and have sweeties on it and it would be big and I would share it with everyone.'

'Sounds like a good cake. You never know, Annie, maybe one day you might get a cake.'

'Nah, I'll never get a cake. My mum doesn't do cakes.'

We continued to play and talk while I mulled over my next task which was to talk to Annie's mum about a birthday cake.

I visited Mum and broached the subject. Her view wasn't so much that her family didn't do birthday cakes but more that they cost too much, she didn't like the taste and anyway what was the point? I suggested that we could bake one together for very little cost and that the point was that Annie really wanted one and it would help her to feel the same as other children.

No amount of talk could change her mind that day. However, on my next visit I asked what Mum was buying for Annie's birthday present. I was told she was getting a scooter. I commented that this was quite an expensive present and asked why they chose to give her a scooter. Mum replied that all her friends had one and she didn't want her child to be different.

'That's interesting, because that is the same reason I gave you for making a birthday cake,' I said.

Before she could say anything I quickly went on to suggest I make a cake for Annie which she could give her. Mum said that if I really wanted to make a cake I could do so and take it into school for her but she was not interested. So I did bake a big cat-shaped chocolate cake and left it at school. Annie loved it and talked about it for a long time, but although happy for Annie I regretted I hadn't been able to persuade Mum to be involved.

The next year I made a conscious decision not to get involved as I couldn't continue to provide a cake for Annie. I wondered what the family would do. I was therefore absolutely delighted to hear that her older sister had home-baked a cake for her and Annie had been ecstatic that her sister had done this for her.

It can be the smallest victories in this job which bring the greatest satisfaction. I hope Annie continues getting birthday cakes.

Creating opportunities to enrich family life

Many of the families we work with are really up against it. Life is a struggle. Parents are coping with poverty, prejudice, and an almost constant presence of the impact of loss, change and unpredictability. Then an outsider comes along demanding change which is rarely viewed as positive by these parents and children. For change is scary so in an act of preservation it is strongly resisted in favour of old beliefs and habits.

I am really only ever working with a family where big changes are required as a consequence of child protection concerns and often when children have already been removed from their parents' care. I know that big changes need to happen but if we can effect some smaller changes along the way which improve life for the children this may assist with the bigger changes. I am mindful that children live in the moment and making small improvements can increase their trust in you, hopefully followed by trust-building with the parents.

It is easy to forget how the simple things in life can seem like the hardest when parents are struggling to cope. Like a trip to the park or the beach. If, as a parent, you have had no experience of such things in your own family life then it is doubly difficult to create positive family experiences. This is why I try to take families out over the summer holidays. It also helps improve the child's life and strengthen relationships within the family and with me. It provides me with assessment opportunities in a different setting. If there are gaps in parenting and childcare they are highlighted when working in a different environment because outings with children can be challenging. Leaving the home requires organisation and confidence and the control of children outside the home can be stressful. Equally, outings can reveal family or personal strengths which might not have been recognised before and can be used to tackle the bigger issues later on. 'Remember how you managed Jimmy when he ran off in the park…?'

Yes, this does take longer than a normal family visit (I usually schedule one and a half hours) but the benefits to the child and to the assessment are significant and justify the extra time.

Practice example

Trudy had two girls, Mary (8) and Hope (4). She had herself been abused and neglected as a child and ultimately had been removed from home. As an adult she had been addicted to heroin but since the birth of Hope had been stable on a methadone programme. Trudy loved her partner, the children's father, Chaz, who had also had an abusive childhood. Chaz was an addict, using heroin, Valium and legal highs and his behaviour was unpredictable. There had been many serious incidents of domestic abuse involving weapons which the children had witnessed. This had brought the children into the protective services and Chaz was supposed to be living away from the home.

I was spending a lot of time with the family, building trust with the two little girls who had been told terrible things about the protective services and social workers and warned not to say anything about family life. I needed to assess Trudy's parenting and build my relationship with her. I was concerned that I might have to take the children from her care as I wasn't convinced that Chaz was really away from the home. Despite his bail conditions not to approach her, I suspected the couple were still in regular contact.

So I organised an outing to the beach. Trudy was keen to go and the children were excited about the idea. However, on the appointed day Trudy had forgotten and the outing had to be cancelled and rearranged for the following week.

I picked them up the next week but in spite of planning with Trudy for her to bring sandwiches and a change of clothing she had forgotten. Anticipating such problems I had necessary spare items in my car, and off we went to a nearby beach. The choice of venue was deliberately chosen as being accessible to the parent so she could return alone with the children.

When we got out of the car I made it clear to Trudy that she was responsible for keeping the children safe and meeting their needs. I asked her to tell me what she understood by this, to check she had absorbed the information correctly. I then stated clearly to the children that Mummy was in charge and I was just there to help Mummy.

As we got organised and the children changed into bathing clothes I immediately noted that Mary took responsibility for Hope and also began to direct Trudy: 'Mummy, can you take the buckets and spades. Hope, you stay here.'

Under Mary's guidance we proceeded to the beach. Trudy sat down on the sand and started to take her shoes off while the children continued heading towards the sea. She was absorbed in this activity, paying no attention to the children.

I called to the children to stop and wait which they did, whilst I prompted Trudy to catch up with them.

The children enjoyed paddling in the water and Trudy did a good job holding their hands and joining the fun. I was able to take a step back and observe from the picnic blanket on the sand, ready to safeguard the children if needed.

At picnic time it was again Mary who took the lead and handed out the food and significantly Trudy appeared comfortable with this. Of concern was the fact that Hope looked to Mary or me for assistance, ignoring her mother.

Afterwards when it was time to play in the sand it was obvious that Trudy had no idea how to play with the girls who increasingly turned their focus to me. Gradually I began to encourage Trudy to become more involved by instructing her.

'Trudy, can you help Mary to dig a big hole and make a moat for the sandcastle?'

'Can you help Hope write her name using seashells?'

Trudy was compliant and enjoyed the play. She began to take over as she engaged with the girls and I was able to withdraw and observe. Ultimately, the children didn't get enough from Mum and began to play on their own. I used this opportunity to talk to Trudy alone about some of the serious issues around the child protection plan. We were able to have a very frank discussion helped by the relaxed location and the fact that she was beginning to trust me.

When the time was up I asked Trudy if she would like me to give her money to catch the bus home, so giving the children longer at the beach, or return with me, and she chose the latter. Ending fun times is never easy with children and Mary made a strong and angry protest. I noted Trudy was not coping with this and she began to waver, looking towards me for help. Even though I had wanted her to take the bus money option, I knew it was important for her to be consistent and follow through with her decision and told her so. The children immediately upped their protests and Trudy sulked, moving into a childlike role. I took charge to prevent the children running off and got them back to the car after 'one last paddle' and some funny songs on the way back.

At the next appointment with Trudy I went over the events of the outing with her. I was pleased to note she was able to reflect, showed a degree of self-awareness and was open to constructive feedback. We repeated the trip two weeks later and I was pleased to see that Trudy had given thought as to how to parent the children. We took some photos to capture a shared happy memory with Mum.

Some tools to teach parents to manage children's behaviour

I guess one of the most common items on parents' agendas is how to manage their children's behaviour and the chances are that if they don't raise it I will. This subject could easily take a whole book (and there are lots of books on the market) but I have confined it to the most common ways I have helped parents.

The most common conversation I have with parents goes a bit like this:

Parent: 'He's a nightmare. He'll no behave.'

Me: 'Can you give me one example?'

Parent: 'He just won't behave. He does nothing I tell him. He'll no listen.'

Me: 'Tell me about the last time you had this problem.'

Parent: 'I don't know. It's all the time.'

Me: 'Okay. If you could just change one thing about his behaviour what would it be?'

Parent: 'That he will do what he's told.'

This kind of circular conversation could go on for hours and be repeated every time you meet the parent if you let that happen. Sound familiar?

The other common statements I hear from parents are along the lines of:

- 'It's no use. I've tried everything. Nothing is going to work.'

- 'Well…I suppose I could try it but it won't work.'

- 'It's no about me! It's her. She's a witch.'

- 'She hates me. She deliberately wants to show me up.'

My task as the social worker is not going to be straightforward. So, when it feels like there is a mountain to climb – use a ladder (Figure 13.1).

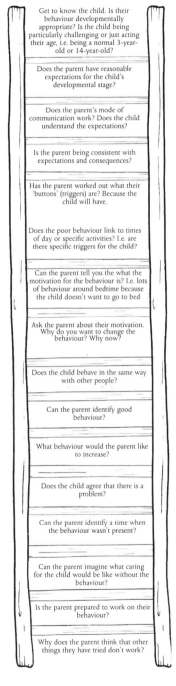

Get to know the child. Is their behaviour developmentally appropriate? Is the child being particularly challenging or just acting their age, i.e. being a normal 3-year-old or 14-year-old?

Does the parent have reasonable expectations for the child's developmental stage?

Does the parent's mode of communication work? Does the child understand the expectations?

Is the parent being consistent with expectations and consequences?

Has the parent worked out what their 'buttons' (triggers) are? Because the child will have.

Does the poor behaviour link to times of day or specific activities? I.e. are there specific triggers for the child?

Can the parent tell you the what the motivation for the behaviour is? I.e. lots of behaviour around bedtime because the child doesn't want to go to bed

Ask the parent about their motivation. Why do you want to change the behaviour? Why now?

Does the child behave in the same way with other people?

Can the parent identify good behaviour?

What behaviour would the parent like to increase?

Does the child agree that there is a problem?

Can the parent identify a time when the behaviour wasn't present?

Can the parent imagine what caring for the child would be like without the behaviour?

Is the parent prepared to work on their behaviour?

Why does the parent think that other things they have tried don't work?

Figure 13.1: The ladder

Assessment activity with the child

You need to find out the child's view of the problem and how they view the parental response. Your questions are:

1. Does the child think there is a problem with their behaviour?

2. Do they understand parental expectations?

3. Do they experience the parent as consistent?

4. Is there a reason for the behaviour beyond normal testing behaviour for their developmental stage?

5. How does the child think we could make it better?

Most children I work with don't respond well to direct questions and will shut down. Use play to help you interview the child.[1] The activities that immediately come to mind are:

- doll's housework (an example is given later in this chapter)

- cartooning

- interviewing the child's soft, or favourite, toys.

So let's assume now that we have a child whose behaviour is based in developmentally appropriate presentation but the parent has not contained this or provided appropriate boundaries, so the behaviour has increased and is now problematic. A simple example would be that a child pushes for a sweet every time they go to the sweet shop (pretty normal behaviour). Typical behaviour from the parent who is unable to contain this would be refusing the request several times but then giving in. The child learns that if he pushes hard enough the adult will give in. It becomes problematic if the child ups their requests in every shop they go into, and the parent always eventually gives in.

Let's further assume that we have a parent who wants to address this and is motivated, even a little bit, to change their behaviour. If you don't have this, then stop as you can't work on changing the child's challenging behaviour when in the care of the parent if the

---

1   For more ideas see Tait, A. and Wosu, H. (2012) *Direct Work with Vulnerable Children: Playful Activities and Strategies for Communication.* London: Jessica Kingsley Publishers.

parent won't accept responsibility. If this is the case you have to work with the parent before you can look at behaviour management.

So, where do we start? The first thing we need to do is increase the parent's awareness of the stages of the behaviour so I introduce them to A B C.

This is:

Antecedent: What was happening before the behaviour started. What was the trigger?

Behaviour: What was the behaviour of the child? And what was the parent's behaviour?

Consequence: What was the consequence of the behaviour? What happened next? What were the pay-offs?

I will talk this through with the parent, filling in the Child Management Chart (Appendix IV) as we go and then leave the chart with the parent, asking them to complete a further three or more examples before I return. I will have established that the parent is confident in literacy. If not they can draw a picture in each column or write one word to trigger their memory for discussion at the next appointment.

I have found people find the behaviour, then the consequence, the easiest to identify and the antecedent often the hardest to work out. The purpose of leaving them to fill in the chart is to:

- help them to reflect on situations

- increase their awareness of the stages of behaviour

- encourage them to take responsibility (not off-load onto the child or worker)

- provide you with an assessment tool and in fact whether it gets filled in or not may help you assess the parent's motivation; the language they use in recording will help you to assess their view of their child as well as their view of themselves.

It is not a particularly easy thing to do and I suggest you have a go at doing it yourself. Look at your own behaviour prior to asking anyone else to do it.

Practice example of the ABC

A parent complained that her daughter just wouldn't listen to her. I asked for a specific example and she told me that she had asked Mary (8) repeatedly not to help herself from the refrigerator. Money was tight and she couldn't afford Mary eating indiscriminately but every day Mary came home from school and raided the fridge. Mum, Tracey, was utterly fed up and increasingly annoyed at Mary's refusal to listen. We decide to apply ABC.

> A: Walking home from school, Mary tells Tracey that she is hungry. Tracey says that she will just need to wait until meal time (two hours later). Mary goes in a huff.

> B: They arrive home. Mary goes to the fridge and helps herself to a yogurt. Tracey yells at her, saying she said no. Mary retreats to the bedroom, yogurt in hand.

> C: Mary eats the yogurt, so her physical need is met but she feels uncontained as she asserted power over the adult.

Tracey has lost control and is angry and upset. These feelings continue on past tea time, impacting on homework and bedtime. No one is happy.

Reviewing the above with the parent, I ask what she could have done differently at Point A. I encourage flexible thinking and problem solving. Many of our parents need a significant level of support for this.

In this case, after long discussion, Tracey agreed there were a couple of possible solutions.

> A: Tracey could provide a small snack before tea time. Tracey could move tea time forward to having an early tea on return from school.

> B: This way the parent is meeting the child's basic physical need and the child is nurtured and satisfied, reducing the need for defiance.

> C: The parent remains in control. No challenge from the child. Potentially this sets a better tone for the rest of the evening.

The significant thing to note here is that in working this way the responsibility for the problem is correctly attributed to the parent and this is done in a non-confrontational manner.

Of course life is rarely that easy and in a few days Tracey was having a new difficulty (or rather a continued difficulty that, on face value, looked new). Mary now said that she didn't want a yogurt or an apple but the packet of cold meat that was in the fridge. When Tracey refused, Mary would help herself and retreat to her bedroom to eat.

Mary had learnt from numerous situations that if she pushed Mum she would gain control. We looked at this with ABC again and Tracey again came up with different solutions at the A stage, but ultimately it helped me to demonstrate to Tracey that the wider issue was a dynamic in their relationship. When Mary was feeling insecure because she was getting a message that Mum could not contain her, she was going to push boundaries at every opportunity until she found a firm boundary which felt safe. Therefore we needed to use some different tools along with ABC.

Tracey suggested a star chart. I have mixed feelings about using star charts so I was in part very pleased Tracey was suggesting a behaviour management technique which showed she was motivated. But the other half of me was concerned as I prepared for some hard work. First I had to repress my own pessimism this would work with Tracey. She found it very difficult to be consistent and had very few resources to draw on as she had experienced very poor parenting herself. Star charts are very simple to use and can be very effective in encouraging positive behaviour or simply getting a child to complete a task. But like so many things it depends on the 'operator' for a successful outcome. If the wrong tone is set, the star chart won't work. If the adult expects too much and the child is unable to achieve what's required, we risk damaging their self-esteem (and the parent feels disempowered too). So there are a few simple Do's and Don'ts when using star charts.

Do

- Do choose to target two or three behaviours at a time and be specific about the behaviour that you want to change. 'Be good at bedtime' will not do, but 'Put your pyjamas on when asked' is achievable.

- Do encourage the child to be involved in drawing up the chart by decorating it.

- Do think carefully about the rewards. They need to be worth working for but also sustainable (I make some suggestions further on).

- Do help the parent to recognise that the action of sticking the star on has got to be accompanied by lots of praise and positive attention and general fuss. This is the child's instant gratification and this is what will make them want to get the next star.

- Do place the chart in a prominent place in the home and at the child's eye level so they can check their progress.

- Do encourage the child to show relatives/friends their chart and encourage people to offer further praise.

- Do be consistent in awarding stars. If you have a goal such as putting pyjamas on, and the child just puts their top on then demands a star, the answer is no, the task is not complete. If two parents are monitoring the chart they have to make sure they are consistent and the child doesn't play one off against the other. Keep the stars out of the child's reach and make a great ceremony of getting them out and allowing the child to pick one and stick it on. This is part of the reward and will make the child want a star.

Don't

- Don't use with children under 4 years. They are rarely developmentally ready.

- Don't have a list of behaviours to be changed which is as long as your arm.

- Don't take a star away after it has been awarded.

- Don't make the reward a huge treat at the end (e.g. buying a games console).

Practice example

Tracey: 'I could use a star chart with her!'

Audrey: 'That's an excellent idea. Have you used one before?'

Tracey: 'It didn't work with me but the school used it with her for her reading and it was really good. She does her reading now.'

Audrey: 'Okay. So Mary knows how a star chart works. Is she still using one at school for her reading?'

Tracey: 'No, that ended before the long holidays, but she was disappointed when it did end.'

Audrey: 'Okay. So what tasks do you think can be on the star chart? Which behaviours do you want to work on?'

Tracey: 'I want her to do what she is telt [told], when she is telt. I want her to stop taking stuff out of the fridge and eating it so I have nothing left for meals. I want her to stop giving me cheek and to get her teeth brushed and hair tied up in a bobble for school.'

Audrey: 'Okay. That's a lot of work. Give me your top three things you want to change out of all that.'

Tracey: 'I want her to do as she's telt. If she did that there wouldn't be a problem.'

Audrey: 'Yes, I get that, but for the star chart we need three tasks. How about we start with, "Brush your teeth in the morning; put hair in a bobble for school and eat snack Mum offers after school and don't eat anything else until tea time"?'

Tracey: 'Aye, that will do.'

Audrey: 'Okay, so what do you have to do to make this work? What about your behaviour?'

Tracey: 'It's not me that won't behave. It's her!'

Audrey, with a smile: 'It's not as simple as that. You are the adult, Tracey. We as adults need to look at our behaviour too – that's parenting. So in order for your wee girl

to brush her teeth in the morning what do you have
to do?'

Tracey: 'Nuthin.'

Audrey: 'What do you need to give her?'

Tracey: 'Toothbrush and toothpaste.'

Audrey: 'She's young, what do you need to say?'

Tracey: 'Go get your teeth done now!'

Audrey: 'Mmm. That might do some days. But do you say it or
shout it?'

Tracey: 'I scream at her. She's so flippin' lazy. Never does
nothing without a good telling.'

Audrey: 'Mmm. Could you just every so often just shout not
scream, "Mary, go and get your teeth done now.
Quickly, I am going to time you. 1…2…3…" Then
when she has finished say, "You were quick. You did
that in 15. I wonder if you will be faster tomorrow?"
Hmmm, I am probably asking you to do something
that's too hard. It's a busy time in the morning.'

Tracey: 'No, I could do that. It's no hard.'

Audrey: 'Really? Aww, that's great Tracey. I am really pleased
you are prepared to try something new. I am proud of you.'

We went through each of the tasks as above, dissecting the
stages and looking at the small detail, discussing what could go
wrong, what might go right and all the time emphasising Tracey's
part in it. I praised, encouraged and enthused throughout. I was
asking her to do things differently. At this point she couldn't
understand the reason for this. Tracey has experienced neglect,
abuse and harsh parenting. This has left her with little empathy
or ability to intuitively understand a child's world. In order to get
her to change her presentation towards her child, I know she
would only do this *because of our relationship*. She would do it

to gain my approval, my attention and praise. So while setting up the star chart with Tracey, I was using behaviour modification techniques with her. I was praising, enthusing and smiling when she described or talked positively about behaviour I wanted her to increase. If she described less positive behaviour I gently corrected and gave less attention. I was also hoping that if I did this enough she would model my behaviour by applying it to her children. I hoped that later on Tracey would become motivated by seeing that she has influenced and can correct her daughter's behaviour.

By the end of this preparation which took two 45-minute sessions we had a list of things Tracey needed to do:

- Make sure toothpaste and toothbrush are laid out for use.

- Don't scream. Use the counting game.

- Praise clean teeth for looking 'sparkling' etc.

- Give a star.

- Let Mary choose her hair bobble.

- Try to relax when doing her hair.

- Be gentle. Don't threaten or hit her with the hairbrush if she doesn't sit still.

- Talk to her about her hair, what she is going to do at school etc. as you brush her hair.

- Give a star once a hair bobble is in.

- Have a snack box at home. Give Mary some choice (go to a fruit and vegetable co-operative or a low-cost supermarket for yogurt). Offer her a drink also.

- After the snack, do homework with Mary or some activity, for example read a book, do a jigsaw etc.

- Allow Mary to help with making the meal.

- Give a star with praise.

In a way we had made an adult star chart for Tracey. I wrote it out as a list and left a copy for Tracey and kept a copy myself. When the star chart had been in place a week I reviewed progress with Tracey, starting with her own behaviour and asked her to rate herself on how well she had done.

Tracey and I had established good rapport and because of her own history, when I reviewed this with her and, using humour, awarded her with little gold stars she responded well. I smiled and laughed with her and she enjoyed the humour even awarding me some stars for social work skills. Again I was creating a modelling opportunity but I wouldn't necessarily do this with every parent. Some would feel it was making light of a difficult problem or experience it as patronising. You have to make a good assessment of the adult and understand the relationship between you and the parent before you use the approach.

Prior to using the chart I did a piece of work with Mary to gain her view of the situation. We used the doll's house (I have a small portable one.) At first we did free play which lasted about 40 minutes. I then explained to Mary I would have to go soon so asked if we could play with the doll's house 'my way' for a short while. Mary agreed.

I took all the dolls out of the house (I left the rooms set up as Mary had done them as she had already told me she was making the rooms and furniture lay-out 'like my own house') and asked her to choose a doll to represent her mummy and one to represent herself. Then, as two of the star chart tasks identified by Tracey were around morning routines I asked her to show me what happens in the morning 'in your home'. She then played out a scene which more or less matched Tracey's description.

I didn't interrupt while she was showing me, but at the end thanked her and commented that it seemed to be a busy house in the mornings with lots of big feelings around. Mary agreed. I then asked, 'Can you show me again a bit you don't like in the morning?'

Mary played out Mum putting the bobble in her hair and we talked about why she didn't like it, how she felt etc. I asked her then what she would like to happen: 'Show me with the dolls how you want it to be.' Mary demonstrated Mummy being gentle and also the child doll getting to choose how the bobble went in – what style she wanted her hair to be in. I noted that to incorporate into Tracey's 'change of behaviour' list.

I talked to Mary about using a star chart and she was keen to do this so at the next session, Tracey, Mary and I made a star chart. Mary decorated it with stickers of her favourite Disney film. Tracey had taken responsibility for buying stars and I brought a fancy tin with rewards in it. I deliberately chose to provide them for the first week as I wanted to show Tracey the kind of rewards that would work. In conversation, Tracey had talked about rewarding with a CD/DVD/cinema trip etc. Personally I felt these rewards were too big. In the tin I placed:

- a new hair bobble and clips

- a small tub of play dough

- a chocolate bar in the shape of a teddy bear

- a packet of stickers

- a bottle of soap bubbles

- a small dog toy.

Only three rewards were required as there were three tasks. However, it is good to give choice. I showed them the box but didn't allow Tracey or Mary to open it and got Tracey to place it in a high cupboard. I explained to Mary that she needed to get seven stars per task for the seven days of the week in order to earn a reward. Potentially she could earn three rewards if she got seven stars for each task. Then she can put her hand in the box with her eyes closed and pick a reward for each star gained.

When Mary was out of earshot I explained to Tracey that part of the reward's success lies not in the monetary value but in the excitement of getting it; praise that accompanies the giving of the reward; and praise and attention that is heaped on the child by Mum telling others about it. All of this is greater than the appeal of the reward. The value in getting the child to close their eyes to pick is two-fold:

- It increases the excitement.

- They will want to work for rewards the following week out of curiosity to find out what is in the box – another motivating factor.

With older children you can vary this activity. Instead of stars on a chart you might award tokens (buttons, dry pasta, stones etc.), placing them in a jar. Ten tokens could equal extra pocket money. You could swap 20 tokens for a trip to the cinema etc. The important thing here though is to have:

Set behaviour = set amount of tokens = set reward.

It is all about consistency.

An example:

Behaviour: comes home at 9pm

Tokens: 5

Reward: 25 tokens = extra pocket money

This can be extended to 70 tokens = a trip to the cinema and so on.

You must be mindful of a child's developmental stage and social circumstances. When you are working out the reward system, some children may not be able to reach 70 tokens, so don't set them up for failure. As a rule, the younger the emotional development the lower the impulse control is, so the quicker the reward is needed. So a developmentally appropriate 4-year-old needs the sticker for the chart immediately when the desired behaviour happens and can wait until the end of the day for the bigger reward. A developmentally appropriate 12-year-old can cope with tokens in a jar and wait until the end of the week or month for the bigger reward.

Some families may not be able to afford to send their child to the cinema so find an alternative. Maybe to choose what to have for tea? Or have control of the TV for the evening? Or go on a bus run? This is surprisingly popular with some of my older teenagers. A day ticket to travel on the bus can produce great behaviour. One of my teenagers loves to travel out to the airport to watch the planes. But again, you need to know your child and to consider safety.

Remember also that star charts lose their sparkle after a while. Usually this is because the parents don't manage to be creative or consistent enough in their praise and the child disengages. It is better therefore to use them effectively for a short while than to try to prolong it and experience failure.

The trick in ending the star chart activity is a skill in itself. It should be used until the behaviour has changed and embedded in the child's day and then removed. I usually do this with a big, unexpected treat/celebration.

For Mary we had a toothbrush and hairbrush party, when she was given new ones. We had cake and balloons to celebrate the fact that Mum and Mary were having 'good times' in the morning. We made a new chart with 'eat snack on the way home and then wait until tea' on it and one new task of 'put on pyjamas when Mum asks'.

After this we changed to tokens and focused on one further new behaviour. Then we had a break from these kinds of behaviour modification techniques.

Tracey needed intensive support during this time in order to follow through on applying star chart work at points. I was having daily telephone calls with her and throughout this work did weekly and sometimes twice weekly home visits. This was not easy work for Tracey but very important. Mary's behaviour needed to change but also and just as significantly Tracey needed to learn new parenting skills to change her behaviour. As a worker I needed to provide a lot of motivation, positive energy, and encouragement, which required personal emotional resources.

On top of that I had to provide firm boundaries and practical resources for both parent and child. Though not easy, I firmly believe in this kind of work and have seen the evidence of how effective and valuable it can be. There were times when I had to dig deep to find the energy to give Tracey and Mary what they needed but this is to be expected. We often work with families who have had very damaged experiences in life. They will often require more than one worker can give, and you may have a number of families to give to. So allow yourself to acknowledge the impact this work has on you and use colleagues and supervisors for support. That is your responsibility to yourself but also to the children and families you work with. If you don't attend to your own needs your practice will suffer.

Reward systems, to be used with behaviour techniques
Star charts

- Up to three behaviours to be listed and stars are awarded with a great fuss and attention each time one of the behaviours is achieved.

- Three stars = reward.

Tokens

This system suits older children.

- The desired positive behaviour is identified and written down. For example, returning home on time; taking a turn to wash the dishes.

- Behaviour has to be specific and achievable.

- When the desired behaviour is achieved, a token (button, bead, plastic counter) is awarded and placed in a jar.

- A set number of tokens = one reward. If you are working with three behaviours you want to change, then the maximum that can be earned in a day is three, one token for each achieved behaviour. The reward is given when three tokens are earned, and this should be a small reward.

- You can also have a ticket system to allow the child to choose either the smaller reward or wait for a bigger one. In other words the child might choose to forgo the smaller reward given for three tokens and save up more tokens for a bigger reward. They can collect, say, ten tokens and exchange this for a ticket which has a bigger reward attached to it. It helps children to have some control and teaches self-awareness.

- So, if using tickets, you could say, 'If you collect 10 tokens [the number will depend on the developmental stage] you will get a ticket. You can choose to use that ticket to get a bigger reward or you can save up your tickets and when you have five tickets [again number depends on developmental age] you can have a Big Treat.'

Colour-in behaviour charts

This only works with children who love to colour in.

- Find a picture of their favourite character, animal or object.

- Buy a new pack of good quality pens. Make it look special so stick stars on it or put them in a nice case.

- Put the picture up on the wall at eye level.

- When the desired behaviour is achieved the child is allowed to use 'the very special pens' to colour in one part of the picture. Note:

  » The desired behaviour has been previously identified.

  » Work on no more than three behaviours at a time.

  » Be specific and make sure they are achievable.

- The adult needs to sit with the child and agree what one part consists of. It could be a girl's dress or an animal on a farm.

- The adult should remain with the child to praise their efforts but also to increase anticipation:

    'I can't wait to colour in that house.'

    'No, you can't do it yet. We will need to wait 'til bedtime and if you brush your teeth you can colour it in then.'

This activity works for two main reasons. The child gets to do something they enjoy and so is motivated to finish the picture and they receive positive adult attention which most children will love. This can be increased by encouraging them to show off their picture to other adults when it is finished.

Collecting a toy system

This system suits children who are developmentally in middle childhood approximately from 5–6 years old to puberty.

- As always the desired behaviour is identified, specific and achievable.

- You buy a toy that has lots of parts. I have used LEGO and similar toys and on one occasion a jigsaw (25-piece). The child loved jigsaws and it was his suggestion.

- Each time the desired behaviour is achieved a piece of the toy is given. A child can earn three pieces a day and the reward at the end is a completed toy.

Some tips:

- The adult should help the child keep the pieces safe until the toy is complete.

- Some children who are used to being given lots of toys and instant gratification will find this reward system stressful so it won't work.

- It also won't work if the adult continues to give other toys for no reason other than to spoil the child.

However, it has worked exceptionally well with a number of children I work with as their motivation to get all the pieces is high because they want a completed toy. Also it works well if they are only used to getting toys at birthdays or special holidays.

I also think it works well with children who don't trust adults to follow through on promises because the child knows the complete toy has already been bought and so the reward is there to be gained.

Chapter 14

Storytelling

Using stories to help vulnerable children manage the impact of loss, change or abuse is not new to most professionals working with children. There are a number of books on the market which go into greater detail on this subject so we would just like to share with you some of the ways we have used storytelling and also to encourage you to try writing or spontaneously creating your own, following a few simple guidelines. We are neither therapists nor psychiatrists but believe that almost any child can benefit from stories covering subjects such as feelings or power and these can encourage more open discussion with the child. More frequently, stories are used to help children process confused life stories and/or removal from home.

Practice example

Bernadette O'Halloran, a senior practitioner in a children and families team in Edinburgh was faced with the prospect of moving a young brother and sister into foster care when their grandmother could no longer manage. The children had had a very disruptive start to life and showed signs of insecure/disorganised attachment. Their mother was a chaotic drug user who had abandoned the children into her mother's care but would continue to disrupt their lives by appearing at unsocial hours banging on the window for attention, causing emotional upset for the children. Understandably, the grandmother and mother's relationship was marked with tension. Grandmother wanted to care for the children but she was not physically fit and not coping. The children were often late for school and nursery and said to be out of control and very disturbed. Strategies to support the grandmother were not effective, even though she loved the children and was trying her best. When Bernadette began to broach the idea of foster care with the grandmother she was very defensive and resistant. However, it soon became clear even to the grandmother that there really was no option and Bernadette was able to identify foster carers and work on a transition plan which involved bringing the carers to meet the grandmother and the children at home and slowly build up contact.

Bernadette's next hurdle was how to prepare the children for the move. She was very concerned about their emotional vulnerability and worried that another move in their early years might prove too much for their emotional states to cope with, and might affect their development negatively. She had recently heard of creative ways of using stories from a colleague, so decided to try something new. Bernadette recalls looking round the office for some play materials she could use and came across some toy horses and farm figures. This provided the context for her story, which would be about two ponies and a 'mother' horse. The ponies represented the children and she was able to find figures to represent the grandmother (even wrapping a bandage round one leg) and the foster carers.

Bernadette recalls that she wanted the story to convey an honest but indirect age-appropriate message. Bernadette thought carefully about the wording and managed to get the children's mother involved, asking her how much she wanted the children to be told about her addiction. From this she created a 'mother' horse who was often 'tired, sleeping all the time, and getting angry'. When it came to explaining why, the children's mother did not want the word 'drugs' to be used and Bernadette was reluctant to use 'bad medicine' in case they ever had to take medication in the future, so she recalls they found something in between. Most importantly the mother, grandmother and foster carers were all on board with the story and later the foster carers were able to use the language of the story when the children asked questions about why they had to move home.

When Bernadette had tried earlier to talk to the children about a move from the grandmother's house, they wouldn't engage and closed off whenever the subject was raised. One child even put her hands over her ears. The first time they heard the story of two ponies 'who had to move stables to keep safe' told to them with the toy figures, they were noticeably happy, engaged and laughing (especially at 'Granny's' bandages). The children immediately identified with the ponies ('that one is me!') and wanted to know what happened next.

During the transition process the story was used by all the adults in the children's lives to help answer questions and address fears. Bernadette feels their mother felt empowered by knowing what was being told to the children and admitted she 'didn't want them to know I am a junkie'. The focus was always on the symptoms and when the children asked their mother during contact some months later, 'When are we going home?' she was able to use the language of the story to explain that she still 'didn't feel well and sometimes got angry' and the children were able to accept this.

The children's behaviour improved markedly after they moved to foster care as they settled into their new home.

Bernadette used metaphor within her story to help the children process change and cope with the strong feelings. In this way she was able to help the children reduce the anxiety attached to the scary prospect of moving to foster care.

Creating your own stories for children is something we can all do. It is also an activity which carries minimum risk. At worst, the child has heard a mildly interesting story with no loss in rapport. Helen was particularly drawn to using stories by what she learned about how the brain works:

1. Our brain needs to know 'what happened next?' which pushes us to seek answers. (To understand this need for the brain to complete the story you just have to think of any time you missed the last five minutes of a film or an episode of a TV drama.) Gaps in our life story can create a yearning to fill that missing piece. This is why life story work is so important. I have come across

children who have created a fantasy story to fill the gap which can prevent them from moving on in a healthy way.

2. The brain is programmed to work out solutions to problems, under the right conditions. Chronic stress will affect this ability. We need to provide the right environment before we can hope to work effectively with families under pressure. Sharing a story is an activity that reduces stress and builds rapport with families. The act of writing a story especially for a family (or child) is in itself a practical demonstration of care which is very powerful and can be instrumental in building positive trusting relationships.

3. We (our brains) are naturally resistant to direct pressure to change (often delivered in terms of 'advice'). Just think of the last time you shared a problem with a friend, who in response said something like, 'Well, you know what you have to do. You have to...' and remember how outwardly you agreed but inwardly you could feel the resistance. This helps us to understand why directives to change rarely work. Sharing a story with metaphor is a gentle way to begin to help people process information and/or begin to accept change.

4. The left hemisphere of the brain is where language and logic are processed. The right hemisphere of the brain is often called the creative side of the brain and has a natural facility to understand metaphor. A story which contains metaphor *and* logic and language uses both sides of the brain. It is even more memorable when visual aids are used, like Bernadette's toy ponies.

Creating your own stories tailored to the needs of the child can give hope, strengthen resilience, help a child to feel good about being different and understand some of the changes that have been pressed upon them. Just the fact you have written a story just for them will help them to feel cared for and perhaps even build their self-esteem.

Some tips:

• Use the same gender and age for the main character. If it is an animal, it can be a boy or girl rabbit.

- Early on, try to mirror the child's own situation. This is the beginning of a story I wrote for a child whose baby brother died from neglect for which, irrationally, the older child was blamed:

    'Once upon a time there were two small rabbits called Davie and Jack that lived in a tiny burrow at the end of a big field near a very busy motorway. Every day they had to run into the big field and look for food, while Mummy and Daddy were sleeping…'

The two siblings (under 3 years) had been left to fend for themselves while parents were in a drug-induced sleep and the younger child died after ingesting medication left unattended.

- Use simple language.

- If the child has particular interests and/or characteristics, bring those into the story and create humour as appropriate where you can.

- Use the story to reframe a situation or embedded belief which is harmful or plainly untrue (the older child was told constantly that he had killed his brother).

- I find it helpful to introduce someone older and wiser who takes notice of the child and reframes the old narrative for them.

- Be careful in your choice of words to make sure you are not unintentionally giving the wrong message. Children are very literal.

- Don't be tempted to end the story with a moral:

    'And so the little bunny rabbit learned never to run near the motorway again/disobey his parents' etc.

If the child asks, 'What happened?' the easiest response is, 'What do you think happened?' in a tone of genuine curiosity. I have been dumbfounded by the insight shown by very young children in response to a story. Remember the brain can process information and look for solutions or clarity in a very creative way. Depending on what you hope to achieve, the story should end by giving hope, a sense of positive things ahead. For my bunny rabbit story I introduced a 'wise old bunny' who noticed Davie was sad.

'Davie told him he was cold and scared because he had made everything die and no one wanted to play with him again. The wise bunny was able to show him that wasn't true. It was the season (winter) which had caused the change and that it only lasted for a while and the trees and flowers would grow again. He then walked with Davie over to a family of bunnies who were playing together in the field…'

Stories should be read in varying tones of voice to match the content and create as much interest as possible. I have read somewhere that using a lower tone than your natural voice adds gravitas to the story, sending a message to the unconscious mind that there is a special meaning within the tale. Storytelling is also a nurture activity, so the children can cuddle up in a blanket or beside their parent to feel safe and cared for.

However, if you feel less confident about writing your own, there are plenty of stories around you can use or adapt for your use. Fairy stories like 'Jack and the Beanstalk'; 'Pandora's Box' and 'The Ugly Duckling'. In Scotland, most schoolchildren know the story of Robert the Bruce and the spider,[1] which teaches children faced with a hard task not to give up, but to 'try and try again'. Within everyone's culture there are similar stories to help overcome adversity, build hope and determination.

---

1   See www.educationscotland.gov.uk/scotlandshistory/warsofindependence/bruce andspider/index.asp.

Chapter 15

Endings

We all face endings in our lives, some more significant than others. Some we look forward to, some we dread. Some we have mixed feelings about but no matter which of the above applies, endings are significant and when working with clients we need to recognise this.

As a newly qualified social worker I often made the mistake, after doing short-term work, of thinking that the family would just be glad to have me out of their lives and while I always made a point of clearly ending my involvement by having a 'last visit' or saying goodbye I didn't really mark the occasion. It wasn't until a few years later when I met some of these clients in the community and they approached me to say hello and reflect on the time we had spent together that I realised that even brief interventions had made an impact and that I should have recognised this and marked the ending properly. Of course for longer-term clients the ending is often quite emotional for both the family and perhaps the worker, bringing a mixture of feelings which have to be worked through.

So, how do we facilitate positive endings? I think of an old-fashioned steam train heading towards a tunnel, each of the carriages representing the stages of an ending. The engine is the family, as it moves forward, the carriages being the different stages of our ending. The tunnel is the place of change where the family goes from being a family with a social worker to being a family without one, emerging from the other end of the tunnel and moving into the future.

In preparing the family (or child/young person) I often use this metaphor with them, drawing it out for them, for the key to good endings is the proverbial three Ps: Preparation, Preparation, Preparation, with a good smattering of ritual and a bit of future planning in terms of what to do if the family wants future support. Or as my tutor used to say, 'Fail to prepare; prepare to fail.'

Endings are a process. People need time to 'get their head around' change, even very positive change. Change can equal stress. Each and every one of us will experience endings at some time. We should never assume to know how the other is feeling about an ending or what the significance of the ending is for them. We should always ask. Some people have never experienced good endings, so you need to challenge yourself to make each ending as good and positive as it can be.

To go back to the train, I draw this for the family on large pieces of paper (see Appendix VI) We can then put it up in the family home, in an area not easily seen by visitors. It needs to be in an obvious place so it can't be forgotten about. It is a visual reminder and helps to keep the family focused on the process. But it's also obviously fairly personal and is not really for viewing by just anyone who stops by. Endings are, after all, also new beginnings and not everyone wants to share their aspirations. One mother said to me when we were discussing her goals, 'I look at them [goals] and I feel strange. When I left school I wanted to be a mother and a hairdresser and go on holiday. Now my dream is to stay clean [drug free] and get myself to the supermarket every week. I really messed up!'

You could view the above statement in a few ways. It could be seen as very sad, and I did acknowledge that but I focused on the positive. I was hearing that statement with some elation because I was standing beside a young woman who could reflect *and* discuss emotion. That filled me with hope – hope that one day she would be a hairdresser and still get herself to the supermarket every week. I shared my reflections with her.

Practice example

I had worked with Marta and her two girls Alice (11) and Kim (3) for nearly three years. We went on quite a journey together. The initial referral came from the police. Marta had consumed so much alcohol she had to be hospitalised. Marta proved to be in denial about her alcohol dependency, refusing to work with the social worker. The children were placed with Granny on a voluntary basis, who then returned them to Marta's care. Child protection procedures were initiated and the children were placed on a register of children at risk and a referral was made to the children's reporter, bringing them into the legal system. At this point Marta acknowledged alcohol dependency and agreed to going into rehab. The children were placed voluntarily with a foster carer until she came out.

Marta reintegrated into the community with the help of family and voluntary agencies and the children were returned to her care gradually. New parenting strategies were consolidated and supports in the community for the children ensured. My involvement with Marta ended one year after the children returned to her care.

Two years after their return home, Marta contacted me for advice. There was brief intervention and then the case closed again.

Once the girls had been home with Mum for about 10 months and there were no concerns in respect of their development or care, I introduced the idea that my involvement would end. I had anticipated that Marta might find this difficult so broke the news to her in a meeting when the children weren't present. Marta was less than happy with me: 'You walk into my life and force me to admit I have an addiction. I sort that out, get the kids back and am just feeling settled and you are going to bugger off! Off to torment some other poor addict, are you?'

I had to stop myself from laughing here. I loved Marta's dry sense of humour and ability to just capture things in a few words. But instead I worked hard at talking about all the positives and why I thought I needed to leave her and the children. To be honest I would happily have been their social worker until the girls were all grown up but that would not have been the right thing for them. During that meeting with Marta the old saying, 'You have to be cruel to be kind', kept popping into my head as well as some self-doubt. Have I judged this timing accurately? Will she be okay?

As we moved towards an hour-long discussion, Marta began to accept the inevitable.

'I never liked you much anyway. Be glad to get my life back.'

Her statements felt like negative disengagement but maybe she just felt rejected by me and was coping with this the best way she could.

I began to talk about the future – the fact that I had no plan to move job and that I would want to hear how they were all doing and definitely wanted to see next year's school photos. (At a later date I ensured that Marta and the girls knew I would understand if they didn't want to be back in touch and that I would not contact them. Any future contact had to be on their terms but right now Marta needed to hear that I wanted to know how they were all getting on. I needed to counter her feelings of rejection. I needed to let her know that I was invested in our relationship, that I cared what happened to her family.)

Marta responded well. I could almost visibly see acceptance. She took a deep breath, 'So when are you leaving us then?' I had a time scale in my head. Six to eight weeks felt right. But I wanted to give Marta as much control as I could. I wanted her to make the decision.

'Well, the longest I can continue to work with you is 12 weeks.' I had deliberately said 12 weeks, as based on previous conversation and my knowledge of Marta she would feel that was too long to wait for the inevitable ending. 'But I want you to decide, Marta. When do you think we should end? What is best for you and the girls?'

After talk and some consideration, Marta said eight weeks. 'That will get us past the school holidays and we will be back to our normal routines.'

I praised Marta on her rational decision-making and commented that this was clear evidence of significant change and progress.

I asked Marta if she wanted me to tell the girls or if she wanted to do this with me present. I was pleased when she said she wanted me to do it. The girls were due home shortly. I explained to Marta that I would tell them about halfway through my session with them and the task before my next visit would be for everybody to think up ideas for an ending.

The girls arrived home and during a craft activity I checked in with them how their day had been and also 'best and worst things since I last saw you'. Towards midway into the session I told them about ending. They both had questions and Alice in particular expressed sadness. We ended our activity and I explained that before I left I was going to draw them all a picture. I drew the train and showed them that we had in fact just done Carriage 1. Could they see what was next? 'Yes, that's right. Plan our ending activity. You start to think about that and next time we meet we will plan it together.' I also gave Marta the task of filling in goals and dreams for the future with the girls. We had done a lot of this kind of work together and I knew she was able. It was a way of me demonstrating to Marta that she could do things with the girls herself. When I first started working with the family I had seen them weekly. More recently I had seen them every two weeks, but this time I made the gap longer and agreed to see them in three weeks.

Next visit I arrived with paper and pens, stickers, snacks and soft drinks. Today was our planning an ending day. There were lots of ideas but in the end the family agreed they wanted the ending to take place in the home. They definitely wanted to do an activity and I was to bring a surprise. I had brought surprises for the girls' birthdays – face painting and balloon modelling. Our activities were generally designed to be fun but also to stimulate conversation around feelings, change and so on. So in effect the activities were the surprise and just pure fun and play. I was interested that the family wanted our last interaction to be similar to our previous work. I had laid out the possibility of going for a picnic or to an ice-cream parlour, which I guess was my perception of an ending, to do something different or special. The family, however, rejected this in favour of the familiar. When I asked

Marta and the children, Marta replied that they enjoyed our sessions and wanted as many as they could have. Between the 'planning the last visit' and the 'ending' visit I met with Marta, Alice and Kim individually. The purpose of this was to give them a slot of one-to-one time in case they had anything to tell me in confidence. It was also a time to make a plan about what they would do if they needed support. Marta had good after-care from the rehab centre. This consisted of a support worker and support groups. She had a good relationship with her support worker and, being an adult, was able to telephone me if needed. In theory I should have directed her to our centralised duty system but I knew Marta would find this hard so as well as telling her the official route to social services I said she could call me. If I could help I would, but if not I would help her to contact the centralised duty service. Martha accepted this and understood that as soon as I stopped working with her family I would be given another family and so might not have space to work with her in the future.

Children are more vulnerable. Alice and Kim were both still quite young with no easy access to a telephone. Both had lots of reasons not to trust adults and it had taken them a lot of courage to build a relationship with me. They were doing well at school. It had been their sanctuary and notably they had never spoken to anyone at school about Mum's alcoholism or being in foster care so I could not assume they would talk to the teachers if they needed support. I also had to apply the same logic to the workers who knew them well in the children's groups. I would of course ask teachers and group workers to monitor their presentation and check in with them but I needed a way for the girls to initiate getting help if needed. So I made 'call cards' for them which simply said, 'Call Audrey, my social worker' with my telephone number. The girls had some in their drawer at home and some in school. In addition I gave them postage-paid envelopes with my name and office addresses on them and a sheet of paper inside. There was a post box on their way to school and we agreed if I got a letter from them I would know they needed help.

I explained to both girls that I would always speak to them but also that they should call 999 (the police emergency number) in an emergency, like Mum drinking again or if they felt afraid. I also explained that I would have other children to look after and so would not be able to be their social worker again but would always be around to help if they needed it. This could include me getting them a new social worker.

This is a very difficult balance to achieve. I needed them to be empowered to ask for help but also to be clear that I had ended my work with them so that they could move on. I was pleased that two weeks after closing the case I received a picture in the post from Alice and Kim. Alice had drawn a picture of her family and Kim a picture of a cat. On another piece of paper Alice had written, 'We are good. Just wanted to send you a picture.'

In case they were testing our safety system, I sent a picture by return of me waving to the girls. I wrote, 'Thank you for your picture' and enclosed some further envelopes and paper. I didn't receive any further correspondence.

On the ending day we looked briefly at the train to focus on dreams and goals. I affirmed that all were achievable. The family had a support worker from a voluntary agency who would continue to work with them. I had briefed her on our train and she would pick this up again. The activity I had brought for our last day was a big cardboard box. We decorated it to make it into a Memory Bank. We filled it with memories of our time together. For the surprise I brought a box of assorted ice-lollies and small water guns. Finally, using a camera with a self-timer, I took a photo of us all together. I posted this to the family about two weeks later along with a card wishing them all well for the future.

Finally

Not all families will relate to trains. You can use any metaphor you think fit. The important elements are:

- You set out the process of endings (e.g. the carriages in my model).
- You acknowledge change (e.g. the tunnel).
- You help plan for the future.

As I said earlier, some people have never experienced a positive ending and it can be a real challenge to make this happen. I guess most of you reading this will be able to think of an adult or young person who, when they know this is getting near, actively disengage as fast as they can and often in a negative way. 'You are going to leave me so I'm going to reject you first.' Of course this response is born out of fear, uncertainty, hurt, loss and is an attempt to gain control and thus feel safe. It is for the same reason that people often work hard at avoiding engaging – they are afraid of relationships which have too often resulted in hurt and loss. This attitude is all about survival. Yes, it is self-destructive and narrows opportunity but for the person taking this stance it is a safer and more comfortable place to be rather than risk loss and hurt again.

These people can prove to be challenging, particularly at the beginning of the relationship. When it is all non-engagement and my hand is sore from knocking on the door and my voice tired from friendly shouts through the letterbox and my diary is under stress from failed appointments it makes the first sign of engagement a joy. The period when you see trust is developing and when you do form a working relationship and enable change makes it all worthwhile and for many social workers it is what keeps us motivated.

But with these individuals and families the endings are just as important as the beginnings. It is all very well that I want to do an ending train – that I think it is positive to have a celebration at the end of our work together, but for some families this is just too much. To make things more complicated there are often competing needs. Maybe Mum can't cope with a planned ending but the child needs it. What do you do?

I have found the best approach is to name the problem. Explain to Mum/Dad and the child or children (if developmentally able to understand) what you think is going on. There are competing needs in families all the time so that is familiar territory. Once you have agreement as to what is happening perhaps think of making a different plan for each person.

But what if you can't even have this conversation as they have already disengaged? Well, you just have to do the best you can. Don't give up after one or two attempts to have a last visit. Try hard! If Mum is not answering the door, could you liaise with the headteacher at school and meet her there to say goodbye and do a farewell visit with the child there? Or link in with health professionals who may still be visiting the family.

Even if these don't work, a card posted to the family is always possible. Don't under-rate this. Cards can be read over and over again and you can write a reflective message as well as positive encouragement. Cards are tangible and you can choose one with a subject that you know the person/family is interested in or one that has a meaning connected with the work you have done together. This gives a subtle message of 'I know your likes/interests and I care'. That alone is hugely important.

Compliment Cards

You care about others' feelings	You get help when you need it	You take part in your community
You're a good friend	If you make a mistake you can say sorry	You work hard at school
You try new things	You are kind	You have good ideas
You're good at football	People like spending time with you	You know how to handle your angry feelings
You are popular	You have a lovely smile	You're good at helping to tidy up
You're strong	You are helpful	People like spending time with you

Chocolate Biscuit Cake Recipe

Ingredients

1 large pack digestive biscuits (500g)

4 tablespoons golden syrup

6 tablespoons drinking chocolate

4oz (100g) butter/butter substitute

cooking chocolate

cake decorations (optional)

You will also need

a big mixing bowl

a jug or bowl to melt things in microwave, or a pan if using a cooker

a tablespoon

a baking tray

access to a refrigerator

What to do

1. Crush biscuits into a big bowl then add drinking chocolate and mix well (a good job for young children).

2. Melt syrup and margarine together. Add this to the biscuit and chocolate mix. (Older teens and adults only as this is very hot).

3. Mix together, working quickly.

4. Place mixture into tray and press down. The mixture is cooler at this stage so everyone can join in.

5. Melt cooking chocolate and spread over the cake with a knife. Add decorations if you are using any. This can be fun for all.

6. Place in fridge to set.

7. Then enjoy!

Appendix III

Rabbit Templates

Fox Templates

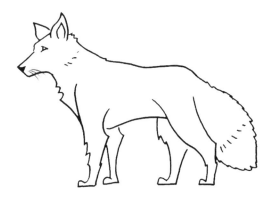

Rabbit Burrow

Appendix IV

Child Management Chart

Antecedent	Behaviour	Consequence

Appendix V

The Detective and the Sniffer Dog Template

Appendix VI

Endings

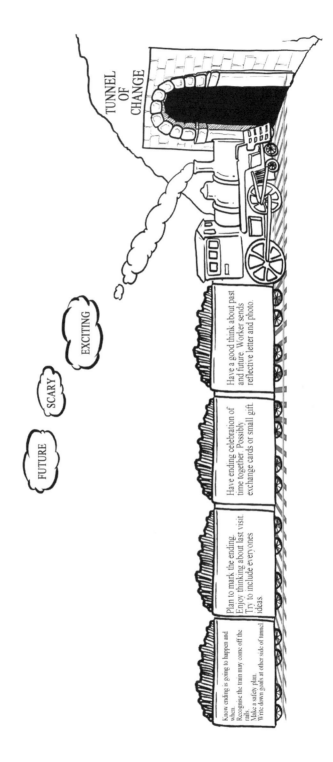

Train Template for Endings

Index

212